Editor:
Robin Jones

Designers:
Libby Fincham, Leanne Lawrence & Tim Pipes

Reprographics:
Jonathan Schofield & Simon Duncan

Group production editor:
Tim Hartley

Production manager:
Craig Lamb

Publishing director:
Dan Savage

Commercial director:
Nigel Hole

Managing director:
Brian Hill

Published by:
Mortons Media Group Ltd,
Media Centre,
Morton Way,
Horncastle,
Lincolnshire
LN9 6JR
Tel: 01507 529529

Printed by:
William Gibbons and Sons, Wolverhampton

ISBN 978-1-909128-03-3

COVER IMAGES

MAIN IMAGE: Bulleid Battle of Britain Pacific No. 34070 *Manston*, which spent many years rusting at Dai Woodham's scrapyard in Barry has, like the Swanage Railway on which it runs, been restored to working order, and is seen heading out of Corfe Castle, overlooked by the magnificent ruins of the medieval castle. Not itself a direct Beeching closure, the branch to the Purbeck resort was axed in the aftermath of his 1963 report and has not been rebuilt from scratch but is now an important local transport provider once again. ANDREW P M WRIGHT

INSET LEFT: Many of the Sixties branch line closures were marked by special events to mark the last train. Ten weeks before the publication of the Beeching Report on March 27 1963, B1 4-6-0 No. 61299, draped in flags and bunting, heads the last passenger train from Pinxton South to Nottingham. COLOUR RAIL

INSET CENTRE: They were destined for the cutter's torch in the Beeching era, but many of the locomotives seen here at Barry scrapyard were subsequently handed key roles in the revival of several closed lines as heritage railways. Nearest the camera is SR U class 2-6-0 No. 31638, later to be preserved on the Bluebell Railway. BRIAN SHARPE

INSET RIGHT: LNER A4 Pacific No. 60007 *Sir Nigel Gresley* takes a railtour over the rebuilt Alloa line on April 24, 2011. IAN LOTHIAN

BEATING BEECH

BRITAIN'S RAILWAYS FIGHT BACK FROM THE AXE

ABOVE: Nature is visibly reclaiming its own as the Stephenson Locomotive Society's 'Scottish Rambler No. 3' railtour stands at Larkhall East on March 29, 1964 behind London, Midland & Scottish Railway 'Crab' 2-6-0 No. 42737. Larkhall East closed to passengers on September 10, 1951, although the Caledonian Railway's Coalburn branch remained open for freight until 1968. Also serving the south Lanarkshire town was the CR's Larkhall Central station, a Beeching closure which succumbed on October 4, 1965. It was officially reopened by the then First Minister for Scotland Jack McConnell on December 9, 2005, when it became the south-eastern terminus of the Larkhall Line, a branch of the Argyle Line, 16¼ miles from Glasgow Central station. In turn, the Argyle Line was created in 1979 as a joint venture by British Rail and the Strathclyde Passenger Transport Executive, reopening most of the Glasgow Central Railway route which closed in 1964 under Beeching. COLOUR RAIL
INSET: The Reshaping of British Railways, a watershed in British transport history. ROBIN JONES

Contents

Introduction

It was on March 27, 1963, that The Reshaping of British Railways, popularly known as the Beeching Report, and a seismic social and cultural shift in the UK of the Sixties, was published.

It marked the definitive watershed between the steam era, the age when railways were the predominant form of public and commercial transport, and modern times, where diesel and electric traction would keep the rail network alive in a world dominated by road transport.

The report was compiled by Dr Richard Beeching, an executive from ICI who had been appointed as chairman of British Railways two years before – controversially on a higher salary than that of Prime Minister Harold Macmillan – in a bid to stem the nationalised rail network's seemingly impossible soaring debts which had reached £120 million.

The document recommended a total of 2363 stations and 5000 route miles for closure and the immediate withdrawal of 250 train services on economic grounds – at a stroke pruning the once-sprawling UK rail network by nearly a third.

As the Conservative government of the day saw it, the situation really was that bad and needed drastic remedies.

Beeching himself did not close any lines, even though the implementation of his first report became popularly termed the Beeching Axe. The recommendations in his report, based on a study of individual lines the previous year, had to be approved by the transport minister of the day, beginning with Ernest Marples who had appointed him. It was the minister's ultimate decision alone as to whether or not to approve or reject Beeching's findings in each case.

Another popular public misconception was that Beeching began rail closures, but nothing could be further from the truth.

Line closures had been steadily under way since the Thirties, and accelerated after nationalisation in 1948. In 1950, British Railways closed 150 miles of track, 275 the following year and 300 the one after that. Between 1954 and 1962, the year before the Beeching report was published, 2380 route miles were closed.

That figure included, in 1959, the Midland & Great Northern Joint Railway route which ran between the East Midlands and Norfolk. That closure sent unprecedented shockwaves through the railway sector, as it was the first time that a complete system, as opposed to a cross-country route or branch line, had been closed.

The swift demise of the M&GN was indeed a harbinger of worse to follow. The focal point as far as the public was concerned was to become the 'bogeyman' Beeching, who has been described as the most hated British civil servant of all time, the man who took our beloved steam trains and branch lines away.

Beeching's report streamlined the closure process that had been under way for more than a decade before his appointment, establishing national criteria for the reduction or elimination of lossmaking services and superseding the piecemeal closure programmes already being implemented by the six regions of British Railways.

Far from setting out to destroy Britain's railway network, Beeching aimed to yank it kicking and screaming into a future dominated by the car and lorry.

His goal was to allow the railways to excel at what they did best while allowing the more versatile road transport to do likewise.

What is so often overshadowed by Beeching's sweeping closures was his huge contribution to the carriage of bulk freight. He introduced the US-style container system which traded under the banner of the hugely successful Freightliner, and modernised coal

ABOVE: British Railways chairman Dr Richard Beeching holds up his controversial report to the press on March 27, 1963. He left the railways in 1965, returning to ICI, and after he retired, he said that one of his biggest regrets was that he did not close more lines. In recent decades, passenger services have been restored to several of the lines that were closed during his tenure and in its wake. NRM

traffic by introducing the Merry-Go-Round system of hopper wagons to replace the ageing fleet of traditional 16 ton coal wagons.

A global phenomenon

The Beeching report has to be looked at in a global context, for it was merely the British response to a transport revolution that was well under way throughout the western world, in which the dominance of rail had come to an end.

Many reasons have been given for the decline of British Railways in the Fifties: the Associated Society of Locomotive Engineers and Firemen (ASLEF) strike of 1955, which crippled the rail network for 17 days – during which time both passengers and freight customers found alternative transport and never went back; the bull-at-a-gate rush to eliminate steam in the wake of the British Railways Modernisation Plan of 1955, which led to the haphazard introduction of first generation diesel locomotives classes, some of which were no better than the steam engines they replaced; the gross overstaffing of stations, and the impact of Marples and his private interests in promoting the road lobby.

Yet the decline in rail use was happening way beyond our shores, and where none of the above factors could have had any impact whatsoever.

The switch from rail to road, branch line closures, rationalisation of networks and dieselisation and electrification had taken off in the USA in the Thirties, and there is little doubt had the Second World War never happened, modernisation of the UK national network would have been accomplished a decade sooner.

Each country tackled the challenge in a different way, but by and large the end results were much the same: the end of steam and a slimmed-down rail network. In Britain, a businessman was appointed from outside its rail industry who could scrutinise its problems with a fresh pair of eyes.

In reality, he was damned if he did and damned if he didn't.

Many rail closures under Beeching led to lasting regret, bitterness and resentment. Yes, the public had their chance to object at their local Transport Users Consultative Committee hearings, but there was a strong sense that in most cases a closure notice was a guaranteed

foregone conclusion. If someone in higher authority wanted rid of a particular line, they would get their way no matter what local arguments were offered in support of the retention of services.

Yet had Britain kept all of its lossmaking lines open, the mood of the public may well have changed within a few years from sentimentality about rural railways to outright anger as they became black holes into which endless streams of taxpayers' money were disappearing.

Macmillan told us we had never had it so good, and the soaring levels of car ownership were testament to that. If a situation arose whereby trains were run empty for most of the day, the public understandably would have demanded to know who was picking up the tab.

Beeching found that just half of the 7000 stations on the network carried 98% of the traffic. A quarter of all traffic started at just 34 stations, while a third of the track was used by just 1% of traffic.

When the Labour Party under Harold Wilson was in opposition, pledges were made that once it came to power, it would sack Beeching and reverse every one of his cuts.

Yet after winning the 1964 election, such promises quickly faded into thin air. Labour not only kept Beeching on and implemented many of his recommendations, but also made other closures over and above those that he had recommended. The reality was that whichever party was in power at the time, the universal approach at the time was that cuts were the only way to stop the losses.

Pruning of the system was therefore inevitable, whether or not it had the name Beeching or that of another person on it.

So with the Beeching report, the walls of the rail empire 'as was' came crashing down.

Once the dust had settled after such a cataclysm, what remained? A network stripped down to the bare bone, with much of the Victorian infrastructure like old station buildings, steam depots and superfluous sidings ripped out, leaving a minimalist but simplified operation in which everything was painted in British Rail corporate blue.

It is a gross understatement that many people were understandably far from happy.

The long road back

The Sixties was the great celebrated era of change, where daily life was changing out of all recognition more rapidly than ever before. Everything seemed up for grabs.

Before then, few people had seriously challenged the establishment. In the wake of the Profumo scandal, Beatlemania, satirical TV programmes like That Was The Week That Was, which dared to take potshots even at royalty, there emerged a greater readiness on the part of the general public to challenge the status quo.

Why should we bow down to the aristocracy? Why should we accept the word of the church and state as gospel? Why should we accept our lot without asking why, and demanding an answer? Added to these was – why should we stand by and let our branch line close?

Lord Stonham, of the National Council on Inland Transport, warned of the Beeching report in 1963: "It will in some areas reduce public transport to a lower level than in the horse age."

There was despondency in towns throughout Britain on the day that the contents of the Beeching report were published in the press. Many communities suspected closures were imminent, but were still shocked at the extent of them. Once they had recovered from the shock, many of them began lobbying and began protest campaigns to save their local lines. Few succeeded.

However, some of the first examples of 'beating Beeching' came not from placard-waving protestors, but from the very establishment which had appointed him.

Beeching had been ordered to look at each line on a profit and loss basis. He was given no remit to consider the wider social ramifications of closures, or any facility by which concerned local authorities could retain services by payment of a subsidy.

Such provisions were introduced by one of Marples' successors, Barbara Castle, in the 1968 Transport Act, which paved the way for urban lines to be run under passenger transport executives which could take social and local transport considerations into far greater account.

By way of balance here, however, it has to be said that Mrs Castle made further closures in the wake of the Beeching report, such as the long and widely regretted Midland Main Line between Buxton and Matlock, even though it had not been listed in the 1963 document for the axe.

In March 1964, a year after the Beeching Report appeared, Marples announced a reprieve for two routes which Beeching had earmarked for closure – Scotland's Ayr-Kilmarnock line and the Central Wales line from Craven Arms to Llanelli. In the case of the latter, he said it was because the sparse communities that it served had no other public transport, but cynics pointed out that it ran through several marginal parliamentary constituencies.

A few weeks later, Marples announced that three more sizeable routes would be spared from the Beeching Axe: the Far North Line from Inverness to Thurso and Wick and the Kyle of Lochalsh branch from Inverness, on the basis that their losses would cause severe hardship to isolated communities.

Then in September 1964, the lines from Llandudno Junction to Blaenau Ffestiniog, Middlesbrough to Whitby and Newcastle to Tynemouth via Riverside were saved by Marples.

In other less fortunate cases, however, local people decided to do it themselves.

Emulating the earlier success of the volunteer-led revival of the Talyllyn and Ffestiniog railways, the Bluebell Railway Preservation Society set out to save the entire Lewes to East Grinstead line as a public transport corridor, but ended up running, initially, the Horsted

Keynes to Sheffield Park 'middle' section as a nostalgia-based tourist attraction.

The Bluebell Railway was the first section of British Railways standard gauge line to be reopened as a preserved railway. Somewhat ironically, in 2013 it completed its northern extension to reconnect with the main line at East Grinstead – the town where Dr Beeching lived in retirement and where a road, Beeching Way, was named after him. The extension was officially opened on March 23 – exactly 28 years to the day after he died in the town's Queen Victoria Hospital at the age of 71.

Many more volunteer-led revival schemes would follow the Bluebell blueprint, with the Keighley & Worth Valley Railway being a classic example of a complete branch line saved by local people.

Yet while Britain today has a magnificent portfolio of 108 heritage lines, how many of them can say that they offer 'real' daily timetabled public transport as opposed to tourist or enthusiast services, despite the original intentions of their saviours?

While many of today's heritage railways boast very impressive annual visitor numbers, they run primarily in the tourist season and cut operating losses by the use of volunteer labour. Their many achievements are truly marvellous, but how far can they be said to have disproved Beeching's calculations that their particular line did not pay?

By the early Sixties, many had sincerely believed that the days of the railway were numbered, and the car and lorry would kill them off just as the railways had quickly eliminated stagecoaches and then, over a longer period of time, the carriage of freight by inland waterways. Indeed, the Beeching closures, drastic as they were, did not end the losses, and passenger numbers on British Rail continued to decline until the end of the Seventies.

The tide turns

It was around the end of the Sixties that local authorities woke up to the fact that road transport was not going to be the whole answer, and the case in future decades would not be as clear cut as the Beeching Report had suggested. Replacement buses had been laid on, but many of their services quickly proved wholly inadequate and withered and died within a few years, leaving rural communities without any public transport.

Opposition to further rail closures now came not only from outside the corridors of power but, as we shall see, inside them as well.

In Chapter 1 is the incredible story of a civil servant who did everything he could to save the Cambrian Coast Line from closure; and in Chapter 2, landmark action of a local council which paid to have services return to the Peterborough-Spalding line a few months after they were withdrawn.

In 1969, there was also the incredible story of an eagle-eyed weekly newspaper accountant who spotted British Rail trying to sneak in a legally required advertisement to close its local line and managed to set the legal wheels in motion to prevent it – Chapter 3.

ABOVE: The magnificent Calstock viaduct carries the Tamar Valley line between Plymouth and Gunnislake. The Callington branch from Bere Alston was listed for closure in the Beeching report but was retained as far as Gunnislake because local roads were poor. Gunnislake became the terminus on November 7, 1966, the service to Callington having been withdrawn the previous Saturday. The surviving branch incorpates the former Southern railway main line from Plymouth to Exeter as far as Bere Alston. In March 2008 Devon County Council backed a proposal by developer Kilbride Community Rail to construct 750 houses in Tavistock, while reopening the 5.5 mile section of this line from Bere Alston to a new station in the town. BEN HARRIS

ABOVE: According to pressure group Railfuture, Dolgarrog was the first station in Britain to be reopened after the Beeching Axe was wielded. An intermediate station on the Llandudno Junction to Blaenau Ffestiniog line which was reprieved by Transport Minister Ernest Marples in 1964 on social grounds, he nonetheless closed the station serving the village that year. However, it soon reopened, on June 14, 1965, and is now an unstaffed halt on what is marketed today as the Conwy Valley Line. NOEL WALLEY*

Today, the North Warwickshire Line is a major commuter route that nobody in power would dare consider for closure.

This book is the story of the different ways in which rail supporters both inside and outside the corridors of power fought back, and the success that they have achieved.

The third in a trio about the Beeching Axe, which follows the earlier *Beeching: 50 Years of the Axeman* and *Beeching: The Inside Track*, also published by Mortons, it looks closely at inspirational stories like these, as well as several of the major initiatives by local authorities not only to restore passenger services on freight-only lines but also to rebuild long-closed routes deemed uneconomic in the Sixties.

Now serving larger areas of population where traffic congestion has reached gridlock levels, their day has come again.

The book also looks in depth at the key role played by the heritage sector, such as the first rail privatisation, in the form of the sale of the Paignton to Kingswear line straight out of British Rail service, and the incredible story of the Swanage Railway, a post-Beeching closure literally rebuilt from scratch by volunteers and which now forms a major public transport hub in the Isle of Purbeck.

One of the greatest successes of the pro-rail lobby was the saving of the gloriously-scenic Settle to Carlisle route, where again, a man in a key position on the inside played a pivotal role. Now, part of another major trunk railway, the Waverley Route, is returning life.

In the Beeching era, Bob Dylan told us that the times they were a-changin'.

Indeed they still are – and a future in which more and more rail closures are being reversed now seems very bright.

Chapter One

The mole within

Beeching was given the job of eradicating British Railways' soaring losses by recommending the closure of lossmaking routes. He was not given any remit to suggest the retention of unprofitable rural routes on social grounds.

Therefore, the 1963 report called for the complete closures of the lines to the north and west of Inverness, the routes to Wick and Thurso and the Kyle of Lochalsh branch. Clearly routes through sparsely-populated mountainous regions could never be made to pay, and they were duly and easily added to 'the axeman's list. It was then left to political pressure to save both routes.

The Celtic fringe in Wales would receive similar attention. Many routes which wound their way through the Cambrian mountains serving isolated farming communities were lopped off to serve the supposedly greater good. The Cambrian Railways main line from Shrewsbury via Welshpool to Aberystwyth and Pwllheli underwent a resurgence in passenger traffic after the Second World War, as the Welsh coast again became popular with tourists.

However, lack of demand was leading to the branches being pruned well before anyone had heard of Beeching. The short Mawddwy and Kerry branches lost their passenger services prior to nationalisation in 1948, and both lines closed completely in the 1950s. The Tanat Valley route to Llangynog began losing its passenger services as early as 1952.

The Beeching Axe led to the Cambrian main line between Buttington (near Welshpool) and Whitchurch closing in January 1965, depriving the Cambrian Coast Line of traffic. While the 1963 report did not ask for the closure of the Shrewsbury-Aberystwyth/Pwllheli route, it eradicated many of the smaller stations and halts.

It appeared that it was being lined up for a second round of cuts. In my earlier volume, *Beeching: The Inside Story*, John Edser, the last surviving member of Beeching's planning team at British Railways headquarters, revealed that one of two cross-country lines in mid-Wales was earmarked for the chop, under the policy of eradicating duplicate lines. It was touch and go as to which would be chosen, and some expected that the Ruabon-Bala-Dolgellau line would be spared, even though it had already been decimated by floods and closed early.

The transport minister decided ultimately that the Shrewsbury-Aberystwyth/Pwllheli route would be the one to be retained.

The route just so happened to pass through seven Labour-held marginal constituencies. It has been said that neither a Conservative nor Labour government would want to bear the burden of closing it, for fear of the electoral consequences, and so it remained open.

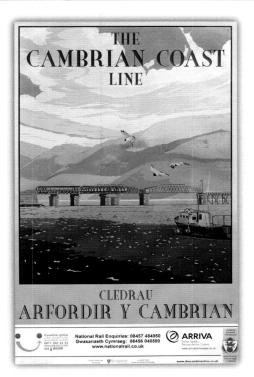

ABOVE: A pair of Class 158 DMUs pass at Tywyn in February 2010. ROBIN JONES

LEFT: GWR 4-6-0 No. 7819 *Hinton Manor* accelerates away from Machynlleth with the 'Cambrian Coast Express' on August 2, 1987. BRIAN SHARPE

RIGHT: A modern-day poster promoting the Cambrian Coast Line, which was so nearly lost. ROBIN JONES

Political pressure saved the day, but there would be another, and another, and another after that, for those who wanted rid.

The closet preservationist

The Cambrian Coast Line serves Tywyn, where its station stands next to the western terminus of the Talyllyn Railway, which in 1951 became Britain's first heritage line, having been taken over by volunteers under the guidance of transport author Tom Rolt.

Joining the growing band of Talyllyn Railway Preservation Society volunteers in 1955 was 33-year-old Reginald Dawson. An RAF volunteer at the outbreak of the Second World War, Reg started as a radio mechanic. He was discharged in 1945 and married his wife Betty in 1946. He then trained as a teacher and rejoined the RAF, where he rose through the ranks to become a Flight Lieutenant in 1960.

Reg left the RAF in August that year having obtained a high-ranking position as a principal civil servant in the Ministry of Transport and was given responsibility for pay policy in the nationalised industries, and met several senior railway managers including the operating superintendent at Euston. He was invited aboard the divisional manager's saloon on several occasions. Reg was now pursuing his interest in railways in his professional career, never turning away an opportunity to become involved with them in the corridors of power.

Labour Transport Minister Barbara Castle, who closed lines over and above those recommended for the axe in the Beeching Report, nonetheless finally brought official recognition to the fact that some unprofitable lines also served a social need. Indeed, as the railways had been taken into public ownership for the good of the people, was it good enough to tell those people who relied on their local trains that they were being withdrawn?

In February 1968, Reg was promoted to lead the division that dealt with grants for unremunerative services. "I was to do the work I coveted and get more money for doing so," Reg wrote later. The Cambrian Coast Line had been chosen the previous year as a test case for this new socially-minded approach. Should it be subsidised – or closed down altogether?

Reg had a vested interest, because at that time, 15% of Talyllyn passengers still arrived by main line train.

He telephoned Richard Hope, secretary and future president of the TRPS, who had just been appointed as editor of *Railway Gazette International*, which was based near Waterloo and a short walk from the Transport Ministry. The pair met for lunch to discuss a strategy to save the line.

The pilot cost/benefit study of the Cambrian Coast Line was being overseen by Australian economist Dr Stewart Joy, and Reg was invited to accompany him on a trip over the route in August 1968. Joy was given a footplate ride on the narrow gauge line into the bargain.

However, on the way home, Joy told Reg that a grant for the line could not be justified in his opinion, and despite Castle's sympathetic stand on rural railways, many officials in her ministry far from agreed with it.

Among their number was permanent secretary David Serpell, who had encouraged

ABOVE: A Class 158 Sprinter runs below Harlech Castle en route to Pwllheli. The Cambrian Coast line links five of the Great Little Trains of Wales, in the Ffestiniog & Welsh Highland, the Talyllyn, the Fairbourne, the Welsh Highland Heritage Railway and the Vale of Rheidol railways.

Beeching to take the job of chairman of British Railways. Serpell is best known for his Thatcher era report on railway finances which was published in January 1983, and included an option to close all but 1630 miles of the country's railways. Mercifully, the Serpell Report died a death, but it did cast light on thinking in some corners of Whitehall.

Reg became aware that he was likely to be moved away from dealing with railways, so arranged a final throw of the dice. He fixed the award of a modest grant which allowed British Rail to resume Sunday services on the line from July 5 to September 6, 1970.

The Talyllyn saw an upturn in passenger numbers on the 10 Sundays over this period, and the increased passenger usage proved a stumbling block in the men from the ministry's efforts to go one better than Beeching and close the route.

Reg, meanwhile, leaked to Richard Hope details of a high level meeting involving around 20 civil servants and held in secrecy. Their aim was to compile an argument for another massive round of rail closures,

without letting on to any MP, not even the transport minister.

Richard approached *Daily Express* journalist Chapman Pincher whose subsequent story was published on May 15, 1970.

That seemed an end to the matter. However, in June 1972, Reg accidentally came across a top secret document called Railway Policy Review. Despite the risk of his cover being blown – all the copies were numbered – he allowed Richard to borrow it, but not copy it.

Secrets revealed as hunt starts for Whitehall 'mole'

Richard knew that without documentary proof, any story about planned rail cutbacks would lack substance. So he copied the document after all. He thought about how to break the story in the strongest possible way, and in the end contacted the *Sunday Times*.

The edition of October 8, 1972 gave huge coverage to the story, and was accompanied by a map of which lines were threatened. The ministry was aghast.

Reg was interviewed by security staff, who by then knew from which office the copy of Railway Policy Review had originated, because a *Sunday Times* journalist who had interviewed British Rail chairman Richard Marsh two days before the story appeared, had handed him a photocopy. Marsh refused to give it back, and it had handwritten notes scrawled over it.

"I came as close to panic as I ever have done during my whole life," Reg wrote. The mole hunters asked Reg if he knew Richard, and he said they were both Talyllyn members and had lunched together in London on October 2. Reg and Richard agreed not to communicate again until the dust had settled.

It was reported in the *Daily Telegraph* of November 14 that the director of public prosecutions had told Scotland Yard to find the mole who had 'borrowed' the blue book. On November 29, Detective Superintendent Croucher and Detective Sergeant Whisker from Scotland Yard raided the *Railway Gazette* office, spending three hours looking for Railway Policy Review. They looked in vain, as it was well hidden.

Richard recalls how the office was shared with *The Railway Magazine*, whose editor John Slater indicated to the officers which filing cabinets belonged to his publication, and were therefore not covered by the search warrant.

On December 7, *Sunday Times* editor Harold Evans was interviewed by police who told him that he and two of his reporters faced prosecution under the Official Secrets Act.

Writing in the TRPS quarterly magazine *Talyllyn News*, issue 236, December 2012, Richard recalled: "Shortly after that we realised that *Railway Gazette* phones were being tapped, not just in the office but also our homes.

"One result was that one of my journalists was visited at home twice by police who threatened to expose the fact that he was homosexual and lived with a male partner. They told him what they had found out by listening in to a call to a friend, proving conclusively that they had tapped his phone line."

Talyllyn member Phil Glazebrook, who worked for the Post Office as a telephone engineer, knew the engineer responsible for the private telephone exchange in the magazine's office block. He showed Richard the bright solder where the tapping wires had been installed.

This time round, it was the turn of the *Sunday People*. It ran the telephone tapping story on December 18, highlighting the fact that police were tapping press telephones without the legally-required Home Office clearance.

Nuneaton's Labour MP Leslie Huckfield, who was believed to have had a conversation with Richard tapped, secured an adjournment debate in the House of Commons.

Meanwhile, Richard was fearful of being jailed for contempt of court if he refused to reveal his source.

The mole wins the day

The Heath government backed down. The attorney-general announced on January 17, 1973 that there was "insufficient evidence to charge anyone". Victory came in July that year. Transport Minister John Peyton told MPs that "draconian cuts of the kind at one time rumoured following the escape of a regrettably mobile document are not in the view of the government the answer to the industry's or the nation's problems".

Two Talyllyn members who had spent their spare time saving a little 2ft 3in gauge in mid Wales had secretly saved an entire main line route, and probably

ABOVE: Class 37 No. 37428 *David Lloyd George* runs along the Cambrian coast at Llangelynen on June 17, 1989. BRIAN SHARPE

OPPOSITE PAGE MIDDLE: The Narrow Gauge Railway Museum at the Talyllyn Railway's Tywyn Wharf station, was awarded Full Accreditation status by the Museums, Archives and Libraries Council in 2012. To celebrate the occasion, the museum operated a special train for volunteers and invited guests on July 11, 2012, with No. 1 *Talyllyn* hauling the line's original rolling stock and three slate wagons, replicating the typical configuration of a Talyllyn train from the line's opening in 1865 until the start of preservation in 1951. TR

ABOVE: Class 31s
Nos. 31147 and 31146 cross
Barmouth Bridge with a
summer Saturday train to
Pwllheli on June 6, 1992.
BRIAN SHARPE

much more. The public outcry over the telephone
tapping and the prospect of another harsh round of
Beeching-style cuts had led to a climbdown which
probably saved many other lines as well.

Reg retired in the Seventies and he and his wife
decided to move to Tywyn, where they continued to
help with the little railway. With their health failing, in
2003 they moved to a warden-controlled flat in
Llandudno. Reg had developed Parkinson's disease and
Betty Alzheimer's.

Richard related how he received a letter from Reg on
September 5, 2012, after a last ride on the Talyllyn,
telling him that they had decided to end their lives at
the Dignitas assisted suicide clinic in Zurich. They died
there peacefully together on September 17.

In the letter, Reg had written: "My most useful action
for the TR was probably to grant-aid Sunday trains on
the Cambrian."

On October 1, their ashes were carried on the
Talyllyn with their four children and their families
present. Only after Reg's death was Richard able to tell
the story of the unsung hidden hero who had rescued
the Cambrian Coast Line and may well have stopped
many more planned closures in their tracks.

The route was threatened once again in 1980 when a
marine worm was found to have badly damaged the
timber viaduct across the Mawddach estuary at
Barmouth. However, local authorities backed British Rail
in funding structural repairs.

The Eighties also saw the introduction of radio
signalling and the replacement of the ageing DMUs. The
last scheduled freight over the line was in 1993. With long
sections of single line and limited passing points, following
further rationalisation of the infrastructure in the
Seventies, minor disruptions on the Cambrian Coast Line
quickly lead to compound delays and partial cancellations.

ABOVE: David Curwen, Bill Trinder, Pat Whitehouse, Tom Rolt and Pat Garland, the well-known 'Five Conspirators' behind the Talyllyn Railway takeover by volunteers, pictured at Tywyn Wharf station in 1971. However, it was a future member of the Talyllyn, Reg Dawson, who would secretly save Tywyn's other line, the former Cambrian Railways Shrewsbury-Aberystwyth/Pwllheli route. TR ARCHIVES

Combined with short turnaround times for rolling stock at each end of the route, it led to severe punctuality problems during much of the first decade of the 21st century. In post-privatisation operator Arriva Trains Wales' performance statistics the route was routinely the worst-performing service group between 2003 and 2008.

In October 2006, it was announced that Network Rail would pilot the European Rail Traffic Management System on the Cambrian Coast Line. "The ERTMS will allow headways between trains using the same track to be reduced without affecting safety, allowing a more frequent service. If the pilot scheme is successful, ERTMS is expected to be rolled out on other rural routes in Britain."

Since early 2009, recorded timekeeping by Arriva Trains Wales' has improved, despite the route being used as a testbed for virgin signalling technology.

Today, trains between Birmingham and the Cambrian Coast line run at an approximate two hour frequency, usually consisting of two two-car units which divide/combine at Machynlleth; one portion continuing to/from Pwllheli, the other to/from Aberystwyth.

The new signalling system and other infrastructure changes will allow the frequency of trains to/from Aberystwyth to double. The Shrewsbury-Aberystwyth/Pwllheli route is unlikely to ever be made to pay, but serving many isolated rural communities, it will take a massive sea change in public opinion to accept its closure at any time in the future.

I wonder. What ever happened to that missing copy of Railway Policy Review? Thankfully, history at least consigned it to a waste paper bin with a double-arrow logo on the side.

ABOVE: Talyllyn Railway 0-4-2T No. 1 *Tom Rolt* and 0-4-2STs No. 2 *Dolgoch* and No. 4 *Edward Thomas* line up in Tywyn Wharf station yard in February 2010. The Cambrian Coast Line runs at right angles immediately behind. ROBIN JONES

B1 4-6-0 No. 61348 at Spalding Town in October 1961, alongside a first generation diesel multiple unit. Built in June 1949 at Gorton Works, it was withdrawn from 38A Colwich shed on Boxing Day 1965 and dismantled by Garnham, Harris & Elton in Chesterfield on February 28, 1966. COLOUR RAIL

Green shoots in tulip country

Lincolnshire did not fare well under the Beeching Axe, with several major towns losing their rail link.

Before the axe fell, the county, the second biggest in England, was served by a near-labyrinthine network of lines, most of which ran through predominately rural and sparsely-populated areas.

The writing was on the wall for several of these routes before the name Beeching was ever spoken at British Railways headquarters. In 1960, the year before his appointment as chairman, British Railways signalled its intention to close the route from Louth to the bustling seaside resort of Mablethorpe and its

neighbour Sutton-on-Sea, served by a loop line off the Great Northern Railway main line route from Peterborough to Boston and Grimsby.

Lop off the branch and soon that main line will wither and die, said many local councillors. They were proved right.

As with so many Beeching closures, a bustling seaside resort meant little. The revenue from the six weeks at the height of the summer season paled against the losses incurred the rest of the year when trains were nowhere near full.

The councillors fought the Mablethorpe loop closure plans, but the resort nonetheless lost its services from October 5, 1970.

Beeching went further. He recommended the closure of the Peterborough to Grimsby main line, and its branch to a far bigger resort, Skegness. The idea was to leave just one railhead – Boston – serving that part of the East Lincolnshire coast.

Local councils understandably objected, and the Ministry of Transport told British Railways to go away and think again. Revised plans were drawn up, much the same as before, but leaving the line from Boston to Skegness in place. And so it remains to this day, the end of the Poacher Line, served by trains from Nottingham via Grantham and Sleaford. The Jolly Fisherman, the classic Great

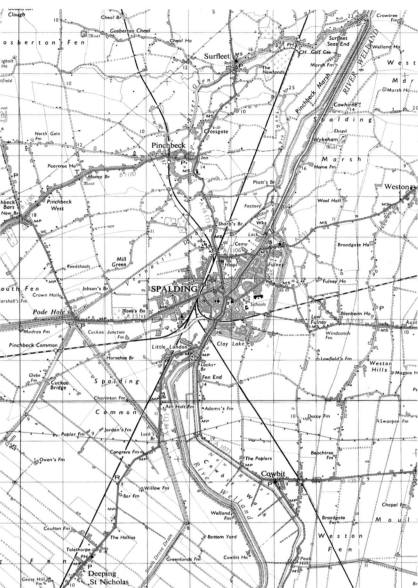

Northern railway advertising poster which told everyone that Skegness was bracing, still beams down from station signs and lampposts, although the mass excursion trains of the steam era come no more.

In the companion volume *Beeching: The Inside Track*, the sole surviving member of Beeching's planning team, John Edser, who worked in the department for several years after the doctor returned to ICI, said that the East Lincolnshire route from Peterborough to Grimsby was one line that he regretted had closed.

Its demise was recommended in the Beeching report, along with the above-mentioned branches. According to John, the rationale was simple: while pruning the railway map down to an inter-city network, Beeching did not want lines doubling up. While the East Lincolnshire line was the most direct to London, it ran through large areas where comparatively few people lived. By contrast, the alternative but longer routes from Grimsby to the capital via Scunthorpe and Doncaster and Newark-on-Trent via Lincoln, where they would pick up the East Coast Main Line.

A succession of battles to save the East Lincolnshire line served only to delay the inevitable result of the Beeching mindset: it also closed on October 5, 1970, the last trains running two days before.

John Edser and countless others now see that times have changed since Beeching did his sums, Had it survived, the East Lincolnshire line would have provided a fast route from Grimsby to London, providing scope for stimulating development en route. As it is, a town like Louth does not have the benefit of a railway, motorway or dual carriageway.

An early spring

Spalding, once the tulip capital of Britain, had been superbly served by railways. Not only was there the East Lincolnshire line to Boston and Peterborough, which opened in 1848, but also the Midland & Great Northern Railway from the East Midlands to the Norfolk coast, linking Spalding immediately to Bourne in the west and Holbeach and King's Lynn in the east. Then there was the Great Northern & Great Eastern Joint Line which ran from Doncaster via Sleaford to Spalding and on to March and Cambridge, built to take Yorkshire coal into East Anglia and opened in 1882. The coming of the railway saw Spalding double in size within half a century.

At its height, Spalding station and its yard had 18 tracks, taking sidings into account, which needed five signalboxes to control.

By the Second World War one of its biggest exports was tulips, shipped out by rail. In 1959, the annual Tulip Festival

ABOVE Spalding was once a significant railway crossroads, as seen from this Ordnance Survey map of 1963. First served by the Great Northern Railway's line from Peterborough, it was later crossed from west to east by the Midland & Great Northern Joint Railway route from the East Midlands to Norfolk, and then also served by the Great Eastern & Great Northern route from Sleaford to March.

was launched, and British Railways cashed in by running excursion trains from all over the country to Spalding.

In 1950 Spalding was still quite a busy railway centre, with an average of 45 passenger trains stopping at the station on weekdays.

That year, however, the death knell for rural railways sounded louder than ever across Britain.

Rail closures had been going on since the Thirties, on a small but piecemeal local scale, but accelerated in the Fifties under British Railways. Every region had seen lines close, but what sent shock waves throughout the whole network was the axing of a complete system, that of the Midland & Great Northern line. Never before had it happened, and it gave a foretaste of what would follow under the Beeching plan four years later.

When the East Lincolnshire route closed, it left Spalding served only by the Great Northern & Great Eastern route. Great if you commuted daily to Sleaford or March – few did – but no good if you needed to reach the regional centre of Peterborough 14 miles away, or Boston.

Beeching had no facility for asking local councils to subsidise unprofitable lines and services to keep them open. That move came under Transport Minister Barbara Castle, under the 1968 Transport Act, when it became clear that there may well be a need for lossmaking branch lines on social and economic grounds.

The closure of the East Lincolnshire line robbed townsfolk of the one route they needed most of all.

ABOVE: BR Britannia Pacific No. 70013 *Oliver Cromwell* storms through Spalding with the 'White Rose' railtour from King's Cross to York on June 22, 2013. ROBIN JONES

ABOVE: Thompson B17/1 4-6-0 No. 61641 *Gayton Hall* and B1 No. 61325 at Spalding Town. No. 61641 was built at Darlington in May 1933 and was shedded at 31B March. It was rebuilt as a B17/6 in 1949. Withdrawn on January 28, 1960, it was cut up three days later at British Railways' Stratford Works. No. 61325 was built by the North British Locomotive Company in Glasgow in June 1948 and shedded at 40B Immingham. Withdrawn on September 22, 1963, it was cut up at Cashmore's yard in Great Bridge, West Midlands two months later, after just 15 years' service. COLOUR RAIL

Thankfully, after sizeable public protests, members of the former Spalding Urban District Council decided that they would have none of it.

In one of the first such rail support initiatives of the post-Beeching era, this local authority came up with a grant to pay British Railways to reintroduce services to and from Peterborough.

This section of the East Lincolnshire line was still in use by freight traffic, and had therefore avoided being ripped up within weeks like so many other lines closed after the Beeching Axe.

Thanks to the council, on June 7, 1970, passengers were once again able to board a train at Spalding and travel to Peterborough for work, shopping, or to change to an East Coast Main Line train to London.

It was a limited service, running only at the peak hours, and just three trains a day. However, the crucial fact is that it was not only running, but it had been reintroduced.

Looking back, the importance of this reopening, small beer as it was in the overall scheme of the national network, cannot be overstated.

The mountain that had stood immovable in the way of many other protests to save or reopen closed lines had here given way, and there was at last a chink in the armour of British Railways' headquarters and its seemingly unswerving corridors of power.

Very small beginnings in the fightback, yes, and it did not lead to anything near an overnight reversal of Beeching cuts, but in the fertile fenland of Spalding, famous for the vivid colours of its spring blooms, seeds had been sown and green shoots had burst forth. A blueprint had been laid out for others to follow, even though most revivals elsewhere would be decades away.

The town has never regretted the council's actions in stumping up that cash.

In 1994, the trackbed of the lifted East Lincolnshire route north of the town to Boston was turned into a trunk road, the A16.

Meanwhile, with the slow decline in freight traffic from the Fifties onwards, the Great Northern & Great Eastern line became under threat too.

Guyhirn and Murrow stations were closed to passengers as early as 1953. Other intermediate stations closed to passengers on September 11, 1961 and to goods four years later. The southern end of the joint line from March to St Ives closed in 1967.

The St Ives to Cambridge section was closed to passenger services in 1970 and the line between Spalding and March on November 1, 1982.

That meant the only passenger trains left using Spalding station were those that ran between Peterborough and Sleaford. Their

ABOVE & LEFT: Spalding station was opened by the Great Northern Railway on October 17, 1848. Even though the company's original route from London to the north had been superseded by what is now the East Coast Main Line within four years, traffic on the East Lincolnshire and later the Midland & Great Northern routes was such that by the end of the 19th century the town had become a major rail crossroads and the station and town had more than doubled in size. It later became a popular destination in its own right, with Spalding's annual Tulip Festival bringing excursion trains from all over the country from 1959 onwards. ROBIN JONES

frequency was stepped up with the closure of the line to March.

Had it not been for the council grant, Spalding today would probably not have even these services. A town of more than 28,000 people would have been cut off from the railway network, because the figures did not add up in the Sixties.

As it is, the once-direct route by rail from Spalding to Boston has been replaced by a circuitous journey via Sleaford. Would Boston not have benefited from a faster rail link to Peterborough and London too, in the 21st century?

In 1975, Metheringham and Ruskington stations between Sleaford and Lincoln were reopened. However, the other intermediate stations between Sleaford and Peterborough have remained closed, despite a good case for rail once again serving substantial villages like Donington, Deeping St Nicholas via the former Littleworth station or Deeping St James, a commuter settlement for Peterborough.

ABOVE: Gosberton station north of Spalding on the line to Sleaford opened in 1882 and closed in 1964. Its former platforms now gone, and looking very much the worse for wear, it has since been in local industrial use, typical of hundreds of closed rural stations across Britain. ROBIN JONES

ABOVE: No. 70013 *Oliver Cromwell* is one of two survivors of the British Railways Britannia Pacific class which were closely linked with East Anglia. Such occasional steam specials as well as regular passenger services still run through Spalding, thanks to the vision of the local council which stumped up a subsidy and gave the route a lifeline in 1971. How many other routes across the country might have been saved if councils had taken a similar approach in the post-Beeching decade? ROBIN JONES

A new public outcry

Clearly the more revenue that a railway line can generate, the more chance it has of staying open, being improved or services being increased.

Pro-rail campaigners and politicians regularly talk about taking bulk freight off the roads for the benefit of all.

That is exactly what has been proposed for the Spalding to Peterborough line, with a new freight hub near the former Littleworth station.

Yet… local residents are up in arms.

The Rail Freight Interchange has been earmarked in the South East Lincolnshire Local Plan for a 37 acre site close to the railway through Deeping St Nicholas.

The plan, which sets out the vision for the South Holland and Boston area through to 2031, also includes an adjoining 112 acres for industrial use.

Villagers are horrified at the prospect of ending up with a massive industrial estate where up to now there have been green fenland fields.

Around 800 out of the village's 1000 residents signed a petition against the rail hub, which they say would turn the village into an urban area.

Protests were intensified in the summer of 2013, months away from a final decision being taken.

Herein lies a new quandary for the powers that be: place industrial development away from railways, and you are accused of worsening congestion on the roads while ignoring the benefit of green transport.

Build it next to railways, as was the case in the early steam age, and you upset the neighbours.

Don't build industrial estates, and the economy suffers.

The road to the future of rail is not as simple as some might want us to believe.

ABOVE: Had it not been for the local council's action in 1970-71 which saw Spalding station reopened for passengers, the post-Beeching cuts might have left the town with only this exhibit at the Tulip Festival as a railway presence. ROBIN JONES

LEFT: Ivatt 'Flying Pig' 2-6-0 No. 43065 at Spalding on February 21, 1959, a class regularly seen on the Midland & Great Northern Joint Railway line through the town. Built at Doncaster in November 1950, it was withdrawn on January 10, 1965 and cut up at Wards of Beighton on April 30, 1965. COLOUR RAIL

GWR 4-6-0 No. 4965 *Rood Ashton Hall* passes Blunts Green north of Henley-in-Arden with Vintage Trains summer Sunday twice-daily 'Shakespeare Express' on June 30, 2013. In many ways, serving small villages and with so much of its original infrastructure surviving, the double-track North Warwickshire Line, which has twice escaped the threat of closure, is all but a heritage railway by the back door. MARTIN CREESE

Break a newspaper embargo,
save a line!

BELOW: Pressing north again: GWR prairie tank No. 5542 heads over the stupendous Stanway viaduct north of Toddington on May 24, 2010 following the relaying of track towards Broadway. JACK BOSKETT

In the build-up to Easter 1969, an accountant at the *Stratford-upon-Avon Herald* weekly newspaper noticed that British Rail had reserved space for an advertisement.

The paper normally came out on Fridays, but the week in question included Good Friday and so it had to appear on the Thursday.

The accountant, Michael Brockington, telephoned British Railways and asked for the copy to fill the space that had been booked.

Bizarrely, for days British Railways refused. Finally, on the Tuesday, nearing the press deadline, Michael again telephoned British Rail, pointing out that the advertisement could not physically be published if the copy was not supplied there and then.

The advertiser saw sense, and produced the required copy.

When Michael read it, he was horrified.

It was a statutory notice detailing all the replacement bus services that were to be laid on following the closure

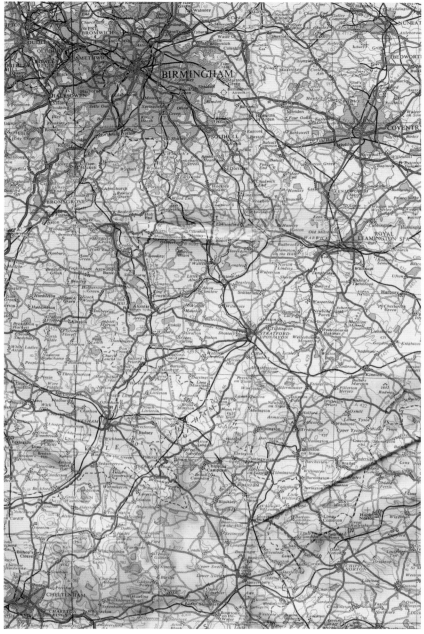

ABOVE: Stratford-upon-Avon's Evesham Place roundabout stands in the way of reinstating the Stratford to Honeybourne line. A tunnel beneath it has been mooted as one way of overcoming this major obstacle. ROBIN JONES

of the North Warwickshire Line between Tyseley, Shirley and Henley-in-Arden and Bearley Junction.

At the time, Michael was secretary of the Stratford-upon-Avon Transport Action Committee, and he immediately saw the implications.

British Rail's closure plans would greatly benefit from publishing the notice just before Easter, when offices would be closed and it would be all but impossible for local people to object to the relevant authorities.

However, they had not taken Michael Brockington into the equation.

In the late Sixties, newspapers were still published using the traditional hot metal process. Michael went into the composing room where the plates for printing were being made up, and did his utmost to get the composers to run him off a copy of the advertisement, three days ahead of it being released into the public domain, as per the agreement with the advertiser.

He then rushed it to Douglas King, a Birmingham solicitor who was acting on behalf of five local authorities, Warwickshire County, Stratford-upon-Avon Borough, Stratford Rural District, Bromsgrove Rural District and Solihull Borough councils, to prevent the closure of the line, its continuation from Stratford south to Honeybourne, from where DMU services would run on to Worcester, set to be withdrawn from May 5 that year.

Beeching had mentioned the 'modification' to the Stratford-Honeybourne-Worcester services in his 1963 report, but made no mention of any intention to close the North Warwickshire Line. However, one of his core strategies in his bid to streamline the system was to eradicate routes which doubled up, and it was also possible to get from Birmingham to Stratford via Tyseley using the main line via Solihull, Dorridge, Hatton Junction, Claverdon and Bearley station.

The threats to the North Warwickshire Line emerged under the subsequent Labour administration. In June 1968, two months after Barbara Castle was superseded as Transport Minister by Richard Marsh, support for the line's complete closure came from none other than Knowle & Dorridge Young Conservatives, whose local station and rail link to Stratford would not be affected.

Birmingham businessman and longtime enthusiast Derek Mayman, the founding director of a successful international company in the construction industry who had become one of the first directors of the Welshpool & Llanfair Light Railway Preservation Company in 1960, mounted a vociferous campaign to save the North Warwickshire Line.

However, at the 11th hour, it was Michael Brockington and Douglas King who found themselves holding the trump card.

Days before the Easter holiday, Douglas King pulled out every stop to obtain a hearing before the High Court went into recess for three weeks. He did so by the skin of his teeth, applying for an injunction to stop the closure.

Michael, who has lived in Welford-on-Avon for the past 40 years, said: "I'm sure that British Rail planned to issue the notice just before Easter when it was too late to do anything about it." British Rail had attempted to close the railway before the replacement bus services had been approved by the Traffic Commissioners.

As it happened, the High Court threw out Douglas King's application, but he immediately appealed, on the grounds that the Transport Commissioners had not agreed the replacement bus services that were listed. On those grounds, he won.

While the Beeching Axe had disenfranchised major towns like Corby, Mansfield and Leek from the rail network, the delightful halts of Wootton Wawen, Wood End and Danzey for Tanworth would continue to service the idyllic rural villages on the North Warwickshire Line.

The injunction remained in place until 1984, when British Rail had it lifted, releasing new plans to truncate the line south of Henley-in-Arden.

By then, the northern section between Shirley, Tyseley and Birmingham Moor Street station had become a thriving commuter line that nobody would then have dared proposed for closure, but south of Shirley, passenger numbers tailed off with the passing of every commuter settlement.

ABOVE: The GWR main line from Birmingham to Cheltenham, depicted on an Ordnance Survey quarter-inch map of 1960, after the stations south of Honeybourne had closed.

ABOVE: Hall Green is one of the busiest commuter stops on the North Warwickshire Line, around which south Birmingham suburbia has spread since it opened. ROBIN JONES

BELOW: Tyseley-based GWR 4-6-0 No. 4965 *Rood Ashton Hall* heads through Wilmcote with a Didcot to Stratford-upon-Avon private charter on July 3, 2008. Express trains were a daily occurrence when the Birmingham to Stratford route was in GWR hands. ANDREW BELL

Many locals immediately saw this new closure plan for the dog it was. If the line was closed south of Henley, it would lose its passengers to Stratford, the primary destination. Therefore, it would be easy to come back in two or three years and claim that there was a huge fall-off in passenger numbers, before cutting the line back further to Wythall or even Shirley.

Michael's successor on the transport action committee, Fraser Pithie, swung into action and rode on the trains collecting around 7000 signatures on a petition.

Eventually, British Rail withdrew the closure notice, after local councils agreed to pay towards the running costs of the four-mile section under threat.

The North Warwickshire Line is a key part of public transport in the West Midlands today. Passenger usage continues to rise, and at Whitlocks End, for long a lonely country halt outside Shirley's urban area, a sizeable park-and-ride car park is often full to capacity, with the modern estate of Dickens Heath a mile away.

Had it not been for a quick-witted rail supporting accountant who was prepared to break a newspaper advertiser's embargo, the region would be so much the poorer for it today.

In August 2013, I had occasion to use public transport to travel to Birmingham city centre and back. I boarded a bus in Acocks Green, estimated journey time less than 25 minutes for 4.5 miles, but which took 10 minutes more. Several years ago, the city council took the decision not to build a dual carriageway through its southern inner suburbs for fear of dividing the communities that lay alongside it. Instead, it followed an 'anti car' approach of narrowing some main roads by adding dedicated bus lanes, with the aim of encouraging motorists to use public transport. The result, in my opinion, has exacerbated gridlock.

Every minor problem, such as a motorist stalling or taking too long to turn right, seemed to lengthen the journey: at times I considered getting off the bus and walking as it would be quicker.

By contrast, a train trip from Snow Hill to Hall Green on the North Warwickshire Line, my next destination and a similar distance, took just 15 minutes – public transport heaven. How on earth could anyone have contemplated eradicating this line – and where would south Birmingham be today if they had succeeded?

In the High Court hearing covering British Rail's plans to close the line in 1969, Lord Denning, the Master of the Rolls, said that while Midland Red had applied to run the replacement bus services, it had "shown no particular enthusiasm about running them". It was also shown the replacement bus services would be slower and costlier, and would not match up with the railway route.

While buses have in themselves brought multiple benefits, in this respect they have been the public transport disaster of the late 20th century. It has been demonstrated that in many cases, within a few years of bus services taking over from trains on a route, services were withdrawn because of apathy from operators, or the lack of willingness to adapt them to fit the exact needs of the communities that had lost their rail link. The net result was that these communities were left with no public transport in any shape or form, and had no alternative but to use the car.

In the Queen's New Year's Honours List 2013, Derek Mayman received the British Empire Medal "for voluntary service to railway heritage in the West Midlands and Wales". Now in his nineties, and still running his business, he can still be seen waving at steam specials as they run past his home near Henley.

The last Great Western main line

The title North Warwickshire line is a misnomer. It lies nowhere near North Warwickshire, and instead partially hugs the western boundary of the county.

It was opened in 1908 as the Birmingham & North Warwickshire Railway, an independent company under the auspices of the GWR.

Laid between Tyseley and Bearley Junction, carrying services which run all 25 miles from Birmingham Snow Hill to Stratford, it provided a double-track alternative to the route to Stratford via Solihull, which was only single track between Hatton Junction and Stratford.

Birmingham's Moor Street station opened at the same time as the line, as a terminus. It served local trains both to Stratford and Leamington, but was closed on Sundays, when all trains ran instead in and out of Snow Hill.

When it opened, it superseded the original branch to Henley-in-Arden from Rowington Junction, which closed to passengers in 1915 and was lifted apart from a short length at the western end which was used for freight.

The Swindon empire had, however, far more grandiose designs for the line than public transport through the growing suburbia of Birmingham and outlying villages in the old Forest of Arden. It was seen as a key section of a new main line from the industrial West Midlands to the South West and South Wales, running via Cheltenham.

After the Midland Railway took over the Birmingham & Gloucester Railway the GWR decided that it needed its own line from Birmingham to Bristol.

Stratford was first served by a steam railway when the Oxford, Worcester & Wolverhampton Railway opened a single-track branch from Honeybourne on July 11, 1859.

It was followed by the Stratford-upon-Avon Railway from Hatton which opened as a mixed gauge single-track line on October 10, 1860. All of the trains were owned and operated by the GWR, which absorbed the railway in 1883. On July 24, 1861, the two lines were linked, forming a through line with trains running from Worcester to Leamington.

The 29 mile southern section from Honeybourne to Cheltenham St James opened to Toddington on August 1, 1904, to Winchcombe on February 1, 1905, to Bishop's Cleeve on June 1, 1906 and to Malvern Road Junction in Cheltenham on August 1, 1906.

The route formed part of a last spate of main line railway building in Britain, which was brought to an end by the First World War. Elsewhere, the GWR stepped up

STRATFORD-UPON-AVON HERALD ISSUE DATED 4TH APRIL, 1969.

ABOVE: On May 19, 2013, Stratford-upon-Avon Parkway station at Bishopton to the north of the town opened seven months ahead of schedule at a cost of £8.8 million. The station, situated near the A46, has 725 car parking spaces, saving passengers from driving into central Stratford to get the train from the existing Stratford station. ROBIN JONES

LEFT: The British Rail advertisement in the *Stratford-upon-Avon Herald* for the closure of the North Warwickshire Line, which sparked off a successful 11th hour attempt to save the route. MICHAEL BROCKINGTON

23

TOP LEFT: Shirley station today thrives as a commuter stop. ROBIN JONES

TOP RIGHT: GWR 4-6-0 No. 4965 *Rood Ashton Hall* powers through the popular commuter station in Shirley with the 'Shakespeare Express'. The station lies a mile from Shirley's centre, but 20th century suburbia sprawled westwards to meet the railway. Its location may have been one of the reasons that British Railways tried to close the line. CHRIS MORRISON

the competition with other rivals by shortening circuitous routes on other main lines, such as London to Birmingham, London to Taunton and west of Plymouth routes.

For the first time, Stratford-upon-Avon found itself on a major main line as opposed to a branch only by local trains. The GWR introduced fast diesel railcars in 1934 between Birmingham and Cardiff, running non-stop via Stratford.

In the 1950s, up to four through trains from the West Midlands ran each day, the most famous of them being 'The Cornishman' which operated from Wolverhampton to Penzance between 1952 and 1962. Peak summer Saturdays saw extra holiday expresses run. Sometimes just 10 minutes apart.

Local passenger services between Honeybourne and Cheltenham were withdrawn as early as March 5, 1960, before Beeching's appointment. As stated earlier, passenger trains between Stratford and Honeybourne were ended in May 1969.

The line continued in use for freight and through passenger trains. Cheltenham Racecourse continued to be used on race days, until March 19, 1976.

Physically, Beeching had left the line intact, but a

derailment at Chicken Curve near Winchcombe on August 25, 1976 brought the axe down.

Reports suggest that after a freight train came off the rails and ripped up a quarter of a mile of track, British Rail moved plant and replacement materials on to the site ready to start repair work – only for workmen to be told that a decision had been taken high up to close the Stratford to Cheltenham route.

In early summer 1979, I watched as demolition gangs lifted the track. It seemed incredible that after the lessons that were beginning to be learned from the negative effects of the Sixties closures, no use could be found for a double track main line.

As it transpired, ripping up the track would be the least of the problems facing future generations who wanted the trains to return.

March of the revivalists

Many local people were extremely perturbed that British Rail had decided to lift the line, and a group was formed with the aim of preventing demolition.

Their efforts proved to be in vain, but in 1981, the Gloucestershire Warwickshire Steam Railway was formed with the aim of restoring the entire route from Stratford to

RIGHT: Western Region Modified Hall No. 7903 *Foremarke Hall* leaves Winchcombe for Cheltenham Racecourse on May 25, 2013, during the Gloucestershire Warwickshire Railway's Cotswolds Steam Celebration marking the reunification of the heritage line following its double landslip calamity. KARL HEATH

ABOVE: In May 2013, LMS Stanier 8F 2-8-0 No.8274 heads a goods train past the infamous Chicken Curve, where a derailment in 1976 led to British Rail abandoning the route between Stratford-upon-Avon and Cheltenham, and where a major landslip in January 2011 divided the Gloucestershire Warwickshire Railway. DAVE GILBERT

Cheltenham with the use of volunteer labour. The revivalists bought the trackbed from Broadway to Pittsville Stadium in Cheltenham, but had been left with no track and many of the station buildings bulldozed.

An operating base was established at Toddington and in 1984, the first public trains ran over a quarter of a mile of relaid track. On April 22 that year, Secretary of State for Transport Nicholas Ridley, performed the official opening.

The railway first extended south, reaching Winchcombe and then Gotherington before a final push to Cheltenham saw Racecourse station opened by Princess Anne on April 7, 2003. The route consists of single line sections with passing places at the major stations.

After starting out with industrial steam locomotive types to haul the early short passenger trains, the railway built up an impressive fleet of main line steam and diesel traction. From next to nothing, it grew in stature to become one of the finest of Britain's standard gauge heritage lines, but could not claim to be running 'real' public as opposed to tourist or enthusiast services.

In April 2010, the line was truncated by a major landslip at Gotherington, and another occurred at Chicken Curve, the place of the infamous derailment, in January 2011. By late 2012, both had been repaired, thanks to the success of a £1 million appeal which was launched by pop music mogul Pete Waterman.

In the meantime, volunteers had continued their push northwards from Toddington to the site of Laverton Halt, giving a running length of 12 miles. It was hoped to reach Broadway, three miles away, by 2015, and from there push on another four miles to Honeybourne, where a main line connection could be re-established.

Honeybourne, which serves the Oxford to Worcester Cotswold Line, was closed in 1969 after the withdrawal of stopping services, but reopened in 1981 in connection with residential development near the station.

Until August 22, 2011 only a single platform face was in use at the station. However, as part of a £67 million project to redouble the Cotswold Line between Evesham and Moreton-in-Marsh and Ascott-under-Wychwood to Charlbury (another route where Beeching stated in his 1963 report that passenger services were to be 'modified'), a second platform face on a rebuilt island

platform was brought into operation for services on the reinstated Up line. Provision has been made for the eventual arrival of the Gloucestershire Warwickshire Railway in the shape of a third platform face on the Down side of the new platform. Once the heritage line reaches Honeybourne, the possibility of incoming charter trains to the tourist honeypot of Broadway or race day specials emerges.

To the north of Honeybourne, around 2¼ miles of track remain. It survived to serve the huge Ministry of Defence Royal Engineers base at Long Marston, which boasted a substantial internal system.

The base has long since closed, and a Gloucestershire Warwickshire Railway splinter group, the Stratford & Broadway Railway Society, was formed to focus on the restoration of the northern section of the route between those two towns. After establishing a base at the MoD depot for several years, the society dispersed, leaving any restoration in the hands of the Gloucestershire Warwickshire Railway.

Through restoration: the brick walls

In 1999, Railtrack plc, a group of post-privatisation companies which owned the track, signalling, tunnels, bridges, level crossings and virtually all of the stations on the British railway system from its formation in April 1994 until it finally ceased to exist in 2002, looked at reinstating the Stratford to Cheltenham line a diversionary route for freight, avoiding the 1-in-37 Lickey Incline. At the same time, Railtrack looked at rebuilding the missing Midland line between Buxton and Matlock, which had been closed in 1968 under Transport Minister Barbara Castle.

Such plans were welcomed by the Gloucestershire Warwickshire Railway, as it would give the revivalists the biggest leap forward in their ultimate goal that they could have hoped for. The plans might have included relaying the second line for Railtrack use, or having freight trains use the single-track line during the week, with heritage services running at weekends.

The plans died with Railtrack's collapse and replacement by Network Rail which, however, continued to support the idea of reinstatement.

GWR 4-6-0 No. 4908 *Broome Hall* climbs the cutting from Stanway Viaduct to Toddington with a Saturday holiday relief working to the West Country on July 25, 1964. THE RESTORATION & ARCHIVING TRUST

BELOW: The first public train to run on the Gloucestershire Warwickshire Railway was headed by industrial Avonside 0-4-0T No. 1977 of 1925 *Cadbury No. 1,* on April 22, 1984. THE RESTORATION & ARCHIVING TRUST

At the Stratford Local Plan public inquiry in December 2003, representations supporting reinstatement of the railway were submitted by Network Rail, Virgin Trains Cross-Country and Gloucestershire County Council among others.

With increasing pressure on the national network to find more paths, surely few should quibble about reinstatement, the sooner the better.

Life is rarely that easy, especially with rail reinstatement.

At the Cheltenham end, the borough council appears to have shown next to no interest in bringing the heritage line further into town, maybe to provide a park and ride to ease the notorious traffic congestion, or better still, reconnecting it to the Main line at Malvern Road junction. Most of the trackbed south of Pittsville Stadium is intact, but in one case a bridge has been removed and replaced by one capable of carrying nothing more than a footpath, and at least one other section of embankment has been allowed to be 'eaten away'

by recent development. However, local residents' potential objections aside, it would not be too difficult to replace the necessary infrastructure here.

The big problem, however, lies at the Stratford end.

Beyond the station headshunt, the formation has been turned into the Summerton Way footpath and cycleway, as far as the Stratford Southern Relief Road, which occupies the old formation.

It has been said that a large grass verge has been left in place so that a single-track railway could be laid alongside the new road. However, since the railway was lifted, houses have been built backing on to the formation much nearer than would have been allowed in railway days, and understandably, the owners have been opposing any reinstatement. Traffic lights and barrier crossings would also be needed, potentially exacerbating traffic congestion in the town.

In 1996, consultant Halcrow Fox surveyed the route and said it would be possible to reinstate the railway through Stratford. Similarly, a more recent study by Arup in 2012 came to the same conclusion, but broadly suggested lowering the railway, dubbed the 'Avon Rail Link', into a concrete cutting alongside the relief road which would be moved over, with pavements on both sides eradicated.

Arup concluded that the line is "a promising candidate for reinstatement", and offered benefits, including additional tourist spend, improved regional rail network resilience and benefits to rail freight traffic.

"It is recommended that the supporters of the scheme seek to attract a rail industry sponsor, promote the project with a range of agencies including Local Enterprise Partnerships, and canvass further support from communities and businesses in the area along the route," the report said.

One big factor is the proposed redevelopment of the MoD base at Long Marston and surrounding land for several hundred houses. Many of the residents may well commute to Birmingham, and a restored railway would help minimise extra rush-hour traffic on the roads.

Furthermore, since 1960, social patterns have changed. Northern Cotswold towns like Broadway and Winchcombe, where few local residents would have needed to travel far to work, are now highly-desirable commuter settlements. Bishop's Cleeve, a village on the northern edge of Cheltenham, is now all but a sizeable town in its own right. Had the railway survived the 1976 derailment, it may well now be thriving.

A restored link through Stratford would also benefit the Gloucestershire Warwickshire Railway, with the prospect of regular steam trips from Birmingham and Tyseley Locomotive Works, the base of Vintage Trains, operator of the summer Sundays 'Shakespeare Express' service.

While many welcome the idea of a through rail route in Stratford once again, neighbouring residents have made their feelings clear. A No Avon Line protest group has already been established in advance of any firm plans for reinstatement.

One solution, I venture to suggest, would be to buy the homes of objectors while paying their owners compensation, and then recoup the money by reselling them, with a covenant precluding future objectors. Reselling homes in a location like Stratford would perhaps not be a difficult exercise.

In the wake of the Arup study, the Shakespeare Line Promotion Group produced its own report which claimed that the railway line could be reinstated for £53 million, 30% less than previously thought. Under its plans, the town centre link would tunnel under at least one road before picking up the old GWR formation on the southern side.

The report stated: "Train services along a reopened rail route could beneficially offer easy and faster travel for residents in the Long Marston and Quinton areas where some 2000 households will reside within three kilometres of a proposed station.

"Overall, there is an unassailable case for the new rail link to regenerate Stratford's tourist economy, secure greater connectivity and environmental sustainability to benefit everyone in and around Stratford."

The report also claimed that local residents would not be inconvenienced by undue noise because of the tunnel and 30mph speed restrictions.

Group spokesman Alan Bevan added: "By eliminating the 'dead end' terminus with a reopened southern rail

link, lots more tourists will be able to reach Stratford from the Thames Valley, Oxford and the Cotswolds."

Herein lies the greatest folly of rail closures, and one for which Beeching cannot be blamed. Axing unprofitable services for which demand has diminished well below break-even level is understandable, as was the realisation of unwanted assets like redundant track.

However, the sale of vacant trackbeds – a factor over which Beeching had no control – has prohibited many potential reinstatement schemes in urban areas, if only because of the insurmountable cost of removing buildings that now occupy them.

If the entire Birmingham-Stratford-Cheltenham line was restored, it would make a splendid commuting and diversionary route, and with tour operator Vintage Trains based at Tyseley Locomotive Works, a brilliant weekend steam highway further enhancing the tourist potential along the way.

TOP: The closure notice that never happened: British Rail giving notice of replacement bus services on the North Warwickshire Line in 1969. The poster was photographed on the wall of derelict Birmingham Snow Hill station in 1976. PETE HACKNEY

BOTTOM: The Stratford southern relief road. Latest thinking is to run the line through a cutting to minimise impact on adjacent properties. ROBIN JONES

The first rail
privatisation

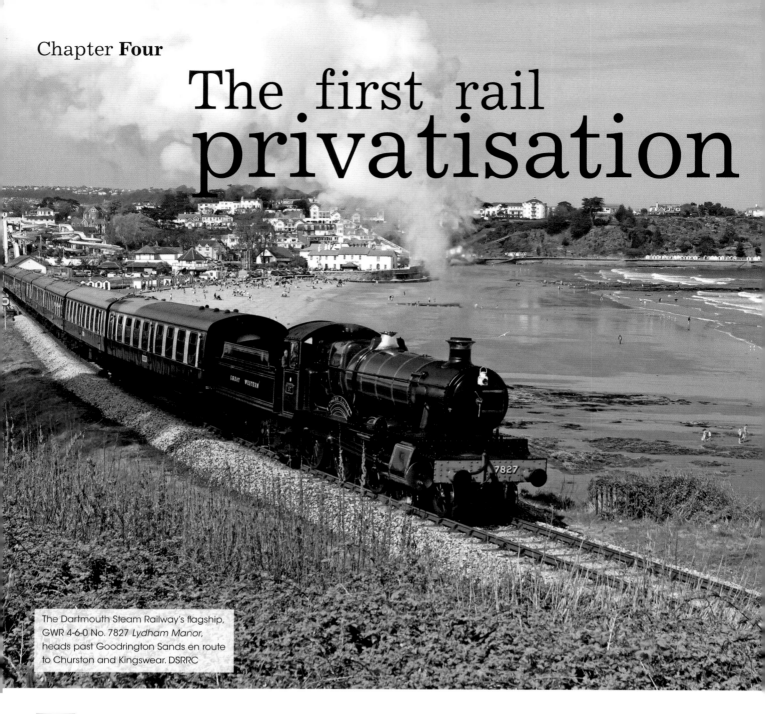

The Dartmouth Steam Railway's flagship, GWR 4-6-0 No. 7827 *Lydham Manor*, heads past Goodrington Sands en route to Churston and Kingswear. DSRRC

The term 'privatisation' as applied to railways immediately conjures up thoughts of the John Major government of the early Nineties, when British Rail was dismembered piece by piece, sparking off a controversy that has endured to this day.

However, the first privatisation of part of the nationalised network, as opposed to the private purchase of a redundant section of line or trackbed for preservation purposes, may be deemed to have occurred as long ago as 1972.

It was then that the Paignton to Kingswear line was sold in service to a private operator. Not only that, but the new owner had British Rail continue to run regular services on its behalf for a brief period.

Beeching barely touched the GWR Paignton to Kingswear route, a seven mile single track 'main line by the back door' as opposed to a classic branch, which extended the double track route to Paignton via Torquay to Dartmouth via a foot ferry.

He recommended the intermediate station of

Churston to be closed, although that was never implemented. Churston was the junction for the short branch to Brixham, which closed on May 13, 1963, not even two months after the Beeching report was published. It had already been recommended for closure, and Beeching merely rubber stamped the decision, and so it never made it into The Reshaping of British Railways.

The pioneering privatisation of the Paignton to Kingswear route had its roots firmly in the preservation sector, although it cannot be classed as a rail revival in the purest sense as it never stopped running.

If railways could run on pure sentiment and enthusiasts' goodwill alone none would ever had closed. Indeed, we would probably have round-the-clock services on the Somerset & Dorset and Lynton & Barnstaple railways today.

Beeching's report was based on brutal hard facts and figures, and it was left to the transport minister of the day, firstly a Conservative one and then his Labour

successors, to make a final decision, taking any extraneous factors over and above the balance sheet into account.

While they might not have been made to pay, people still loved steam trains and rural branch lines, but no other private operator seemed prepared to buy and take over a loss-making line, in an age in which the motor car seemed the only way ahead. Indeed, in the Beeching era, few businessmen would have had the chance if they had wished to do so, as the tracklifting began often within a day or two of the final service, so convinced were the powers-that-be that closed lines would never be needed again.

However, the stunning scenery of the Paignton to Kingswear route presented a different case altogether. Serving Torbay, the heart of the English Riviera and still phenomenally popular as a holiday destination despite the later advent of cheap overseas package deals, it could not only carry passengers but as a steam railway in a world

taken over by diesels and electrics become a major attraction in its own right, especially on those days when wet weather drove holidaymakers off Torbay's red sand beaches. Seaside and steam – an enticing combination indeed.

Mighty oaks from small acorns

The story of how the line – which was not recommended for closure until years after Beeching had left – began with the closure of the GWR Moretonhampstead branch on February 28, 1959, when Collett 0-4-2T No.1466, subsequently preserved at Didcot Railway Centre, hauled the last train.

The Rector of Teigngrace, Canon O M Jones, and Torquay enthusiast E G Parrott established the South Devon Railway Society, attempting to copy the blueprint of the Bluebell Railway founders, whose line ran its first public services in 1960.

The society campaigned for the reintroduction of passenger trains to Moretonhampstead. On June 6, 1960, the society organised a Paignton to Moretonhampstead special, 'The Heart of Devon Rambler', which carried

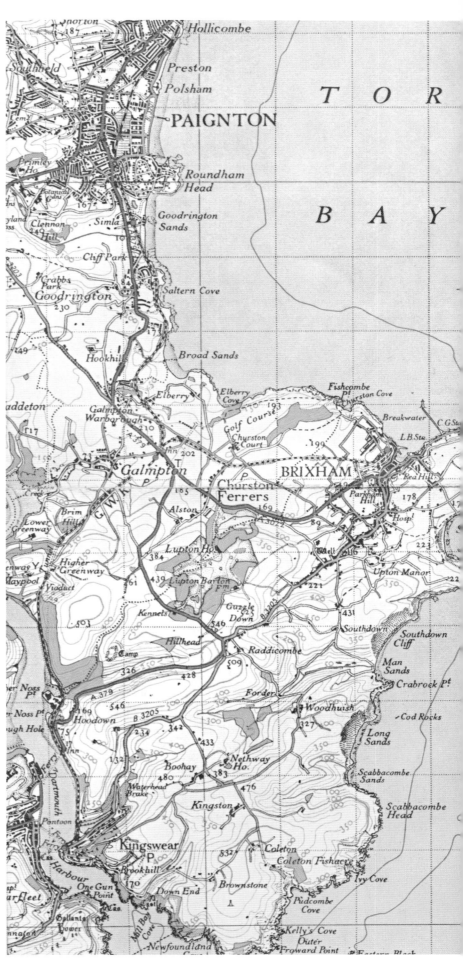

ABOVE: The Paignton to Kingswear line and its Brixham branch as portrayed on the Ordnance Survey one inch map of 1946.

ABOVE: An early Beeching era closure was the Brixham branch, which lost its services in 1963, two months after The Reshaping of British Railways was published, but previously earmarked for the axe. A Brixham-bound auto train headed by GWR Collett 1400 class No. 1452 is seen at Churston station. BEN BROOKSBANK*

more than 200 people, and shortly afterwards, leased Teigngrace Halt as its headquarters.

They were years ahead of their time, and lacked resources to do more. They could not prevent the northern part of the branch beyond Bovey Tracey from being lifted, although the southern part was retained for freight, and much of it survives in occasional use today.

The battle may have been lost, but the society volunteers had learned much from their experience, and looked at other branches which might be saved.

First to come into focus was the GWR Kingsbridge branch, the Primrose Line, which ran from South Brent along the valley of the River Avon, serving Gara Bridge, Loddiswell and Avonwick.

The passenger service last ran on September 14, 1963. The campaigners won the backing of Kingsbridge Town Council only to leave the meeting on September 25 and find the demolition gangs had already begun ripping up the track.

It would be third time lucky.

The GWR branch from Totnes to Ashburton, which closed to passengers in 1958 and freight in 1962, was then considered, and would-be rescuers Bob Saunders and Peter Stedman brought together a group of businessmen including John Evans to reopen it.

However, it would not be an attempt to reintroduce the public services that had been lost, but to revive the branch as a profit-making tourist attraction.

RIGHT: GWR 2-8-0T No. 4277, named *Hercules* by the railway, following a policy of making its locomotives appeal to younger family members, crosses Broadsands Viaduct at Goodrington. DSRRC

Group members saw that within a handful of years, steam trains would be no more, yet there would be droves of tourists who would be prepared to pay to relive times past. They were right, but such revivals cannot be held to have proved Beeching, his predecessors or successors wrong: a living linear steam museum is a different animal when compared alongside a railway running a regular all-year-round timetabled public service.

The Dart Valley Light Railway Co Ltd was set up to buy the line and acquire suitable locomotives, the first arriving on October 2, 1965. From the outset, the operation of a profit-making concern was the basis of the company's business case, and the company has remained true to it to this day.

It was on April 5, 1969, the same year that the branch was bought from British Rail, that none other than Dr Richard Beeching officially reopened the line from Buckfastleigh to Totnes. And yet, as a tourist attraction in a popular holiday destination, it was an overnight success.

Sadly, neither the company nor the preservation movement as a whole was able to stop the northern length of the line, from Buckfastleigh to Ashburton, being swallowed up by the Ministry of Transport's new A38 trunk road from Exeter to Plymouth, despite widespread local opposition to the loss of this section, Instead, all that could be done was the conversion of Buckfastleigh from a through station into a terminus, leaving seven miles of classic GWR country branch line, services run by small tank engines and auto trailers.

ABOVE: Hauling the summer Sunday 'Torbay Express' back to Bristol Temple Meads on July 14, 2013, GWR 4-6-0 No. 5029 *Nunney Castle* leaves Kingswear, with Class 47 diesel D1916 behind, because of Network Rail restrictions on steam locomotives during the heatwave that month which had seen other steam charters elsewhere banned outright. DAVID HUNT

A closure beyond Beeching

At one time, it would have been inconceivable that any of the line between Newton Abbot and Kingswear would have been under threat.

After the First World War, as increasing numbers of working-class families took summer holidays by the sea, the line became so busy on summer Saturdays that in 1930 extra sidings had to be added as storage space for trains, and the running line was doubled as far as Goodrington Sands Halt. More carriage sidings were opened in 1956 at Goodrington, with a turntable installed the following year, and Kingswear signalbox received a new lever frame in 1960.

Beeching may not have had Kingswear in his sights, but the slow rundown of the line south of Paignton would soon be felt. Freight traffic from a wharf at Kingswear ended when it was closed on May 4, 1964, with ordinary goods traffic withdrawn on June 14, 1965.

After April 18, 1966, most Paignton to Kingswear trains were run as shuttle services, apart from in the peak season. The line lost its Sunday trains from September 24, 1967, although some resumed during the summer of 1968. The crossing loop at Churston was closed on October 20, 1968, along with the signalbox at Kingswear.

In November 1968, it was formally proposed that the line from Paignton should be closed entirely.

That was not Beeching's doing, as he had gone by then, but the action of Labour Transport Minister Barbara Castle, who refused to close the St Ives and Looe branches in Cornwall, after commenting on their picturesque nature.

The closure did not happen immediately, and a series of talks to save the line took place.

In 1972, Terry Holder, a former director of the *Economist*, was appointed as managing director of Dart Valley Railway plc. In view of the success of the Totnes to Buckfastleigh steam operation, he saw that there were even richer rewards awaiting if the coastal route could be bought.

Sir William McAlpine, one of the early investors in Dart Valley Railway plc, recalled paying BR £150 to hire a DMU to ride the length of the line to inspect it.

"This was a thing that could not be missed. It was a line which could take the very biggest locomotives, and we were worried that it would compete with the Buckfastleigh line."

Shock waves resounded through the preservation movement when it was announced that the Dart Valley Railway had bought the line on December 30, 1972 – with daily timetabled services continuing

ABOVE: A driver and fireman's view of Goodrington's glorious red sand beach. DSRRC

uninterrupted. For the final two months of the year it had paid British Rail to run DMU services over the line.

The line thereby became the first operational passenger-carrying section of the national network to be de-nationalised.

The total purchase price of £275,000 included the whole line and most of the Kingswear waterfront including the Royal Dart Hotel. Along with other surplus land assets, it was subsequently sold off by the company to recoup much of the purchase price. In short, Paignton-Kingswear was the railway bargain of the century.

Seasonal running saves the day, but…

In the Beeching era, British Railways never tried to deny that many seaside branch lines were exceptionally busy during the summer season.

However, any profits were offset by very poor local usage during the rest of the year, during which the carriages needed to cater for the summer boom in traffic had to be laid up and maintained.

The Dart Valley's experiment of continuing to run local trains throughout the year quickly came to an end that autumn.

Dart Valley Railway plc had learned one lesson the hard way. There was a reason why the minister had wanted rid of the line, and that was because it could not pay.

There was no subsidy allocated to the company to run all-year-round local services.

The way ahead was clear. Run the line purely as a tourist attraction, like any other heritage railway, and forget about 'real' services. There would never be another winter timetable.

The experience brings many of the arguments about Beeching closures and rail revivals into focus.

Under the terms of their original enabling acts of parliament, railway lines would not be permitted to close down for the winter months, or run just for the peak summer season.

Even if they were allowed to do so, it would seem highly unlikely that many local residents would lock their cars in their garages and switch to train travel for the brief part of the year that services were available, and again, the cost implications of mothballing rolling stock

during the winter would be high. A heritage railway, however, running under light railway legislation which permits a maximum of 25mph running, can tailor its timetable to suit public demand. It can choose not to run during times when few people would want to travel, but cherrypick the times when demand is anticipated to be high.

Years before Beeching's appointment, the question was repeatedly asked – does the revenue from the peak summer season cover the cost of maintaining a line throughout the rest of the year? Beeching, like others before and after him, quickly saw it did not.

While many today employ paid staff, heritage railways survive primarily because of volunteer input from enthusiasts who are prepared to give their time free of charge to carry out tasks from ticket collecting to engine driving and laying permanent way. The national network cannot benefit from an army of free labour like this.

There are examples of heritage lines running 'real' public trains for the benefit of local people, commuters, shoppers or schoolchildren, but even where they exist, they are far outweighed by enthusiast or tourist services.

No doubt many a resort would in summer benefit from the reopening of a railway branch line lost in the Beeching era to relieve town centre traffic congestion while bringing more visitors in – Sidmouth, Lyme Regis, Perranporth, Withernsea, Hunstanton and Mablethorpe are a few that quickly come to mind.

Yet how far could a local council justify spending sufficient sums of money to rebuild a lost branch if it were to see basically six weeks' busy use each year but have to employ at least some staff all the year round, if only for maintenance purposes?

A different criteria obviously applies in urban areas where freight-only lines, and trackbeds where they survive unblocked, can be brought back in use to beat road congestion on a daily basis, no matter the season nor the weather.

The tourist transport hub

For years the newly-privatised Kingswear line, which started out as the Torbay Steam Railway, was marketed as the Paignton & Dartmouth Steam Railway, but following a 21st century change of focus, is now known as the Dartmouth Steam Railway & Riverboat Company.

Dart Valley plc eventually bought two River Dart boat companies, added a vintage bus service from Totnes to Paignton and offered the public a unique 'round robin' steam, boat and bus trip experience.

Capitalising on its unique position where river and sea meet, it now runs boat trips to Teignmouth, Torquay and as far afield as Salcombe, where it also operates the Salcombe-Kingsbridge ferry.

As of 2013, it now operates a paddle steamer, the *Kingswear Castle*, which as its name suggests, is part of the heritage of the Kingswear line and the railway.

Built for the GWR in 1924 by Philip & Sons of Dartmouth for service on the River Dart, the ship was chartered to the US Navy during the Second World War, and was used for carrying stores and personnel at Dartmouth. In 1965 *Kingswear Castle* was withdrawn from service and was bought by the Paddle Steamer Preservation Society two years later.

Following restoration, *Kingswear Castle* re-entered service again, operated by the Paddle Steamer Kingswear

ABOVE: Temporarily masquerading as scrapped sister No. 7800 *Torquay Manor* to mark the 150th anniversary of the Dartmouth and Torbay Railway reaching Churston from Torre and Paignton, GWR 4-6-0 No. 7827 *Lydham Manor* arrives at Goodrington Sands with the 4.15pm Kingswear to Paignton service on May 29, 2011. DAVID HUNT

33

Castle Trust based at Chatham Historic Dockyard at
Chatham in Kent. On December 18, 2012, *Kingswear
Castle* returned to the River Dart, under charter to the
Dartmouth Steam Railway and Riverboat Company, to
again run passenger trips around Dartmouth Harbour
and up river to Totnes.

Dart Valley general manager Andrew Pooley has been
busy developing the railway as a transport hub where, just
as in the days of steam, tourists arrive by train and explore
much of South Devon without having to resort to the car.
The railway offers an Oyster card-style Waverider ticket
covering up to three days travel on its boats and trains.

Firmly in the black

The Dartmouth Steam Railway holds a unique position
among Britain's portfolio of heritage lines. It has 120
paid staff and few volunteers, yet it is the only heritage
line that manages to pay a dividend to its shareholders.

A survey showed that 50% of Dartmouth Steam
Railway passengers came back year after year. A *Sunday
Times* survey placed the railway above Blenheim Palace,
Warwick Castle and the Tower of London in a chart of
Britain's top 100 attractions.

Not only does it make a profit by not running trains
through the winter months, but it is a major contributor
to the economy of the Torbay area.

Kingswear is also a popular destination for steam
charter trains running over the national network,
bringing in upwards of 500 passengers at a stroke.

If the line closed, as the Miniastry of Transport had
intended, it is now recognised that the towns along the
route would be so much the poorer.

On the other side of the coin, it is doubtful that if the
line resumed public transport services 365 days a year,
without any public subsidy, it would do anything but
quickly sail into the red. In recent years, there has been
talk of developing Churston station as a park-and-ride
for Brixham, where modern housing estates preclude the
restoration of the original branch. As outlined in
Chapter 17, the idea was included in a 2009 report by
the Association of Train Operating Companies.

The idea is that peak-hour commuter services could
be run to Newton Abbot or Exeter, by an outside Train
Operating Company, without risk to Dart Valley plc but
with the potential to boost profits.

Yet again however, it would surely be a case of
cherrypicking services rather than running a fully-
fledged public timetable, underlining Beeching's stance
that unprofitable routes cannot survive 52 weeks a year
just by running only the profitable services.

PAIGNTON SOUTH DEVON GWR

GUIDE POST FREE FROM DEPT. P. ENTERTAINMENTS MANAGER, PAIGNTON

In September 2013, a plan to create an intermodal road-rail freight terminal on sidings at Goodrington station, serving Torquay and Brixham harbours as a way of promoting short sea shipping, was a surprise inclusion in Tor Bay Harbour Authority's newly-published port masterplan... even though railway officials knew nothing about it and local residents were less than enthusiastic.

It may not happen, but the idea is indicative of the way in which old railway routes are being looked at afresh for unlocked potential. Dart Valley discarded its original line in the early Nineties. In the Seventies, the Buckfastleigh line had been the main concern, and the Kingswear Torbay line was of secondary importance.

However, under Dart Valley plc, the Buckfastleigh line never improved on the 120,000 passengers carried in that first season, and by the late Eighties was seen as a drag on resources. After it was threatened by closure, it was taken over by the Dart Valley's volunteer supporting association and rebranded the South Devon Railway.

In 2010, the volunteers completed the purchase of the line's freehold, and today it's a thriving heritage railway, with no pretence of offering public transport.

ABOVE: The Dartmouth Steam Railway not only offers exhilarating coastal panoramas but stunning estuarine views too, as it approaches the Kingswear terminus. GWR 4-6-0 No. 7827 *Lydham Manor* is seen passing Britannia Halt. DSRRC

LEFT: The long success story of the Paignton to Kingswear since it became the first part of the nationalised rail network to be privatised has seen it branch out into running boat companies and buses too. The latest addition to its fleet in 2013 was paddle steamer *Kingswear Castle*, which was originally in GWR service locally, and so its welcome return to the Dart estuary has seen a wheel turn full circle. DSRRC

Chapter Five

The fall and rise of
Birmingham
Snow Hill

For schoolboy trainspotters, Birmingham Snow Hill was a veritable cathedral of steam. The Great Western Railway's main station in Britain's second city, it had everything any follower of the Swindon empire could wish for, from Kings and Castles down to pannier tanks.

The early Sixties at Snow Hill were a halcyon era for linesiders. I know, for I was there. Before our family had a car, a day out on the platforms at Snow Hill would be the highlight of a summer holiday, otherwise spent spotting on the platform at Widney Manor station on the line running south to Leamington, or at Bentley Heath level crossing, under the auspices of my elder brother.

At the age of six, it was a thrill to enter the great tunnel which led beneath the city centre into Snow Hill from the south, and emerge into steam locomotive heaven. There, you would not have to wait up to half an hour for the next number to add to your Ian Allan locospotter's book; here, locomotives came fast and furious. There was never a dull moment in the non-stop passenger and freight action of one of the busiest stations outside London.

In the summer of 1963, I cared nothing for the name Beeching, whose report had made headlines that March. All that mattered to me was the present, not the future: the glamorous gleaming new Western Region diesels and diesel multiple units and the plethora of steam locomotives, many of which were baked in layers of grime so thick that the cabside numbers were barely visible. Yes, the winding down of the steam age was by then very much under way and in symbolic terms, the writing was very much on the wall in Beeching era graffiti.

Neither did it occur to me to ask why Snow Hill was so busy, or why it was preferred by trainspotters to the rival London Midland station, New Street.

Indeed, at the time, Snow Hill was, temporarily, far busier than New Street, but it would be an Indian summer that would within a matter of years pale into a long cold winter.

The Modernisation Plan

On December 1, 1954, the report known as Modernisation and Re-Equipment of the British Railways, or the 1955 Modernisation Plan for short, a blueprint for the future of the national network, was published, nearly seven years before anyone had heard of Dr Beeching in connection with railways.

Its core principle was the total elimination of steam haulage, and the rapid introduction of diesel and electric alternatives. By the standards of other Western countries such as the US, it should have been published and acted upon many years before, but Britain had been left all but bankrupt by fighting the Second World War and steam was left to reign supreme because of the colossal cost of replacing the railway network's infrastructure.

A major keynote of the Modernisation Plan was the electrification of trunk routes… beginning with Euston to Birmingham, Crewe, Manchester and Liverpool.

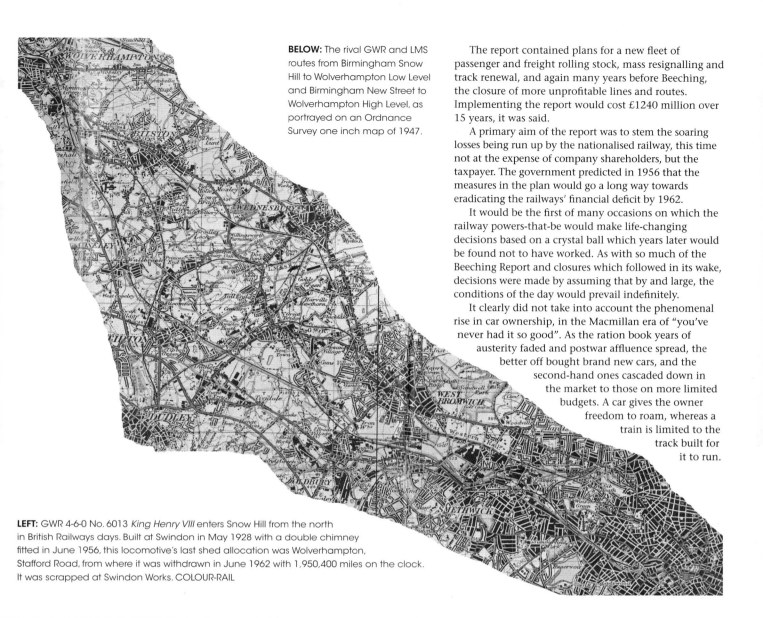

The rival GWR and LMS routes from Birmingham Snow Hill to Wolverhampton Low Level and Birmingham New Street to Wolverhampton High Level, as portrayed on an Ordnance Survey one inch map of 1947.

The report contained plans for a new fleet of passenger and freight rolling stock, mass resignalling and track renewal, and again many years before Beeching, the closure of more unprofitable lines and routes. Implementing the report would cost £1240 million over 15 years, it was said.

A primary aim of the report was to stem the soaring losses being run up by the nationalised railway, this time not at the expense of company shareholders, but the taxpayer. The government predicted in 1956 that the measures in the plan would go a long way towards eradicating the railways' financial deficit by 1962.

It would be the first of many occasions on which the railway powers-that-be would make life-changing decisions based on a crystal ball which years later would be found not to have worked. As with so much of the Beeching Report and closures which followed in its wake, decisions were made by assuming that by and large, the conditions of the day would prevail indefinitely.

It clearly did not take into account the phenomenal rise in car ownership, in the Macmillan era of "you've never had it so good". As the ration book years of austerity faded and postwar affluence spread, the better off bought brand new cars, and the second-hand ones cascaded down in the market to those on more limited budgets. A car gives the owner freedom to roam, whereas a train is limited to the track built for it to run.

LEFT: GWR 4-6-0 No. 6013 *King Henry VIII* enters Snow Hill from the north in British Railways days. Built at Swindon in May 1928 with a double chimney fitted in June 1956, this locomotive's last shed allocation was Wolverhampton, Stafford Road, from where it was withdrawn in June 1962 with 1,950,400 miles on the clock. It was scrapped at Swindon Works. COLOUR-RAIL

ABOVE: Snow Hill station on April 26, 1957. A GWR King has arrived with the 7.30am Shrewsbury to Paddington express. BEN BROOKSBANK*

It soon became apparent that for a family of four, a few gallons of petrol were cheaper than four return tickets.

The national rail strike of 1955 did much to force people from the train to the car.

Days after Anthony Eden's Conservative government won a General Election victory, the union representing train drivers in Britain, the Associated Society of Locomotive Engineers and Firemen, called a strike over a pay dispute, demanding a miniscule pay rise amounting to around the price of an extra packet of cigarettes a week.

The strike lasted from May 28 until June 14, and brought British industry to a standstill and cost the railways around £12 million in lost revenue.

It was a salutary lesson that the unions would take decades to learn, and some of their leaders perhaps never will. Just as the trade union movement had its roots in groups like the Tolpuddle Martyrs who came together out of raw necessity to fight tyrannical employers who cared little if they reduced their workforces to little better than legalised serfs or slaves, so by the mid 20th century, there were an increasing number of incidents when they too were seen to wield power, just because they could. Was a national strike really justified for such a scant reward?

By then, the public was no longer reliant on public transport, as modern alternatives for travel were widely available, in the form of the bus and the car.

Once they switched to road transport because the trains they used to get to work and the shops were not

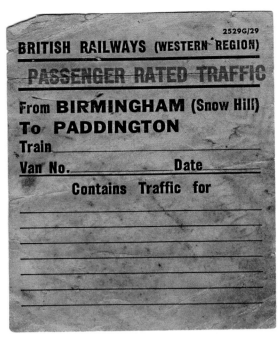

BRITISH RAILWAYS (WESTERN REGION)

PASSENGER RATED TRAFFIC

From **BIRMINGHAM (Snow Hill)**
To **PADDINGTON**
Train_____
Van No._____ Date_____

Contains Traffic for
_____
_____
_____
_____
_____
_____
_____

ABOVE: A luggage label found strewn around the floor of the office on platform 7 at Snow Hill in late 1969. Through trains from Snow Hill to London Paddington had ceased two and a half years earlier. PETE HACKNEY

TOP: The former Great Western Hotel stood at the front of Snow Hill station, and was converted into railway offices after guests said that the noise of freight trains passing in the tunnel below kept them awake. It is pictured in an early 20th century hand-coloured postcard, when electric trams still ran through the city streets. Trams will return to the city centre when the Midland Metro is extended from Snow Hill.

ABOVE: GWR 74xx 0-6-0PT No. 7424 *Snow Hill* with a freight train on February 13, 1963. BILL WRIGHT

running, they found it was more affordable and convenient. Unlike the General Strike of 1926, this time there was another way.

Not only passengers but freight customers switched from rail to road, and after the strike was over, many never went back.

Such social changes would have happened anyway, as evidenced by the pattern throughout the western world. Therefore in that respect, it is probably unfair to single out trade unions as a single cause, but nonetheless history records that it did happen that way.

The Modernisation Plan, based on the premise that for the most part people would still consider train travel as the preferred option, did not reverse the losses, even though vast fleets of diesel locomotives were displacing steam. Eventually, Transport Minister Ernest Marples brought in a non-railwayman from the world of private industry and commerce to sort out the mess and make the railways pay for themselves. The name Dr Richard Beeching would soon be as indelibly marked on the history of Britain's railways as those of Isambard Kingdom Brunel, the Stephensons, George Jackson Churchward or Sir Nigel Gresley, even though for very different reasons.

While British Railways remained in uncertainty and turmoil as the Modernisation Plan was implemented, bucking the trend was the route that had been selected for electrification, the West Coast Main Line.

Although it was not completed until 1974, the project to electrify Euston to Glasgow started in 1959,

when British Railways was still building its final Standard steam locomotives.

The massive cost of replacing the steam infrastructure and installing the 25kV single-phase overhead system meant that it could not be done overnight. Hundreds of bridges had to be altered or replaced entirely to accommodate the overhead wires.

The first length of the newly-electrified line was Crewe to Manchester Piccadilly. It was completed on September 12, 1960, followed by Crewe to Liverpool on January 1, 1962.

Meanwhile, such extensive rebuilding impacted on services along the line. Many were diverted on to alternatives routes… including Paddington to Birmingham Snow Hill.

The first electric trains out of Euston ran on November 12, 1965, with a full public timetable beginning on April 18 the following year. The line to Coventry, Birmingham New Street and Wolverhampton High Level followed in March 1967.

In 1966, a new set of high-speed long-distance services over the route launched British Rail's InterCity brand, offering revolutionary new schedules from Euston to Manchester or Liverpool in two hours 40 minutes.

The northern section was completed on May 6, 1974, with the electrification to the Preston to Carlisle link, bringing in travelling times between London and Glasgow that would never have been possible in the steam age.

From cinders to Cinderella

One of the key planks of The Reshaping of British Railways was the creation of fast inter-city services, and the electrification of the West Coast Main Line was therefore right up Beeching's street.

What wasn't, however, was the GWR London-Birmingham-Wolverhampton Low Level route and its northern 'extension' to Birkenhead Woodside.

To Beeching, that was a clear-cut case of doubling up. In cases where two routes led from city A to city B, he wanted to eradicate the lesser of the pair, or at least downgrade it to local stopping trains only.

The route which went through areas with the higher population or which served major areas of industry would likely be the one to be saved. In the case of Birmingham, it would be the most modern of the two routes, and the choice was clear cut: in fact, it had been made in the decade before his appointment.

Snow Hill would go. Meanwhile, it could bask in the sunshine of its final surge of prosperity while New Street was completely rebuilt in the early Sixties, to an ugly utilitarian concrete design which saved nothing of its Victorian splendour, let along its trademark Queen's Hotel.

Demolition of the old New Street and hotel began in 1964, and the new New Street opened in 1967.

That marked the beginning of the end for its GWR rival on the opposite side of the city centre.

The history of Snow Hill

The GWR had hoped to use the London & North Western Railway's Curzon Street station as its Birmingham terminus, but political manoeuvring between the companies meant that did not happen.

Instead, a site previously occupied by Oppenheims Glassworks was chosen, with the GWR station, a basic wooden structure covering the platforms, opening in 1852. Trains from the south arrived through Snow Hill Tunnel, built by the cut-and-cover method, and in a cutting from Temple Row to Snow Hill.

It was first known as Birmingham, but its name was subsequently changed in rapid succession to Great Charles Street station, and then Livery Street station. It became Snow Hill in 1858. Five years later, the Great Western Hotel was added, and in 1871, a permanent structure was completed.

TOP LEFT: The sign the GWR would never have displayed: in early 1967, Snow Hill passengers are told to use New Street station if they want to go to London. BILL WRIGHT

TOP RIGHT: Snow Hill station on March 5, 1967. The last day of the Paddington services. BILL WRIGHT

ABOVE: The rusting hulk of once-proud Snow Hill station in 1975. PETE HACKNEY

The new station had two through platforms, and bay platforms at the Wolverhampton end, covered by an arched roof. The Temple Row cutting was roofed over in 1872 and the Great Western Arcade built on top.

The station was rebuilt for the second time between 1906-1912 to ease traffic congestion. Designed to compete with the more illustrious New Street, the rebuilt station had a large booking hall with an arched glass roof, and luxurious waiting rooms with oak bars.

The main platform area was covered by a large glass and steel overall roof. It consisted of two large island platforms, with four through platforms, and four bay platforms for terminating local trains at the northern end.

The main line route running north out of Snow Hill towards Hockley was quadrupled at the same time, but the cost of widening the twin track Snow Hill tunnel at the southern end was considered prohibitive. There was insufficient capacity through the tunnel to accommodate all of the services running north into Snow Hill, and so a third city terminal station was built at its south portal. Birmingham Moor Street station was intended as an 'overflow' station to handle local trains running between Leamington Spa and Stratford-upon-Avon. At the same time, the Great Western Hotel was closed because guests complained of being kept awake by freight trains running underneath. It was converted into railway offices, and a passenger entrance was provided on Colmore Row, which became the station's new main entrance instead of the one on Livery Street.

In its heyday, Snow Hill handled many services that today run through New Street, such as those to Shrewsbury, Chester and Mid Wales, and from Birmingham to Cheltenham.

Once the new New Street was open, and the West Coast Main Line offered a faster means of getting from London to Birmingham, Snow Hill's redundancy notice was served.

Beeching had returned to ICI by then, but long-distance services through Snow Hill ended in 1967.

The last train through Snow Hill tunnel ran on March 2, 1968. Local trains serving Leamington and Stratford were then terminated at Moor Street.

The services from Snow Hill to London, the West Country, Stourbridge and Shrewsbury were diverted to New Street, and the branch to Dudley was closed. Services from London still used the GWR route via Oxford and Leamington, but at Bordesley used a loop line to climb on to the Midland Railway's Camp Hill line from King's Norton, before swinging west on to the electrified main line at Proof House Junction to run into New Street.

All that remained at Snow Hill was a shuttle service of four trains per day using Class 122 railcars running north to Langley Green, along with six daily stopping services to Wolverhampton Low Level.

Snow Hill was left as a pale shadow of its former self of a few years before. British Railways steam had gone, the last cinders from the fireboxes had long since been thrown out, and the handful of diesel railcar services did not entice the next generation of schoolboy trainspotters, if there was one.

In March 1972, these last services were withdrawn and the station closed, along with the lines through to Smethwick and Wolverhampton. All that remained of the GWR route from Snow Hill to Wolverhampton was a single line from Smethwick West on the electrified route to Coopers Scrap Metal Works in Handsworth for freight use only.

There was a local outcry when the former Great Western Hotel was demolished in 1969. It later transpired that the standard of the foundations was not what it might have been.

Ironically, the mouldering station became used as a city centre car park, commuter vehicles being parked between the once-busy platforms.

Most of the station was pulled down in 1977 after the dangerous state of the building was revealed. The ironwork of the station roof was badly corroded in several places, and the unstable ground and foundations on which the station had been built were causing it to slide downhill.

A mere handful of artefacts, including the original gates and booking hall sign, was saved and later used in the restoration of Moor Street station.

TOP: By early 1972, Snow Hill was described as the biggest unstaffed halt in Britain. The remaining DMU service to Wolverhampton Low Level was all that remained in service. A Class 122 railcar waits to depart in February that year, shortly before these services were withdrawn. GEOFF DOWLING

ABOVE: Snow Hill busy serving commuters – as a car park, pictured on December 31, 1974. PETE HACKNEY

TOP RIGHT: History comes crashing down: the demolition of Snow Hill station in 1977. DAVID ROSTANCE

ABOVE RIGHT: The year before the bulldozers moved in: Snow Hill station in 1976. PETE HACKNEY

Rebirth

It may have gone, but traffic congestion in Birmingham grew steadily worse through the Seventies as car ownership increased. The track may have been lifted, but the potential strategic value of the lost route as a rail corridor for future commuter traffic was not forgotten.

The West Midlands Passenger Transport Authority adopted a policy to restore cross-city rail services through Snow Hill, easing congestion both on local roads, and also at New Street station.

A new Snow Hill station rose from the ashes of the old. It was by no means as grandiose as the GWR Edwardian one that had been flattened, and was a far simpler and more functional affair, largely covered by a multi-storey car park.

Snow Hill tunnel was refurbished, and the new Snow Hill opened on October 5, 1987, but handling only local services to the south, to Leamington and Stratford.

Up to then, these had terminated at Moor Street. After Snow Hill come on line again, these services instead ran on through the tunnel, and the former terminal platforms were closed.

Six years later, London-bound services came back to Snow Hill.

Network SouthEast reintroduced two-hourly limited-stop services to London in May 1993. However, they were routed to Marylebone instead of the original destination of Paddington.

It was a winner. Soon, the frequency was increased to hourly at peak periods. Chiltern Railways took over the service after privatisation and it continues to this day.

On September 24, 1995, the first northbound trains out of the new Snow Hill ran, to Worcester via Kidderminster. The line ran between Smethwick West and Snow Hill, along with new stations at Smethwick Galton Bridge, The Hawthorns and Jewellery Quarter. Some Chiltern services continue beyond Birmingham to Kidderminster.

The Midland Metro

Although there are regular services between New Street and Wolverhampton, the GWR route that 'doubled up' would also be given a new lease of life... as a light rail tramline.

Birmingham's last conventional street tram ran in 1953. As in other major cities throughout Britain, trams were phased out after the Second World War because buses were considered to be more versatile.

As road traffic levels in the West Midlands conurbation soared from the Fifties onwards, there was much talk about building a light rail system along the lines of those in European cities.

It was in 1981 that the former West Midlands County Council and the West Midlands Passenger Transport Executive, now known as Centro, formed a joint planning committee to seriously consider light rail as a way ahead.

A report, Rapid Transit for the West Midlands, appeared three years later and outlined plans for a £500 million network of 10 light rail routes which would by and large run along streets, but would have underground sections in Birmingham city centre. One of the suggested routes would have used the old GWR route from Snow Hill to West Bromwich.

The big flaw in the report was that it would have involved converting existing rail routes to tramways. For instance, the North Warwickshire Line would have been converted as far south of Shirley, again raising the long-resisted spectre of losing services beyond there to Stratford.

Local people power defeated the scheme. The first route was to have run from Five Ways eastwards across the city centre to Castle Bromwich... and would have involved knocking down 238 properties. Such was the opposition that the WMPTE could not find an MP to sponsor an enabling Bill.

ABOVE: The entrance to Snow Hill station today. ROBIN JONES

The West Midlands County Council was dissolved under the Local Government Act 1985 and after it ceased to exist the following year, a new Passenger Transport Authority was established.

The blueprint for a new light rail scheme under the banner of the Midland Metro appeared in 1986, with a different set of as many as 15 routes.

The first route was announced in February 1988. It would run between Birmingham and Wolverhampton, mainly utilising the disused GWR trackbed.

An Act of Parliament authorising Centro to build the 12.5 mile line was passed in 1989.

A contract for the construction and operation of what became known as Line 1 was awarded to the Altram consortium, a company owned by John Laing, Ansaldo and National Express. The contract was received in August 1995, with building starting three months later. Finished 10 months late, the estimated cost was £145 million.

ABOVE: The Midland Metro Line 1 route map. The line mainly follows the old GWR route from Birmingham Snow Hill to Wolverhampton Low Level. CENTRO

ABOVE: Midland Metro tram No. 4 stands at the Snow Hill terminus on August 23, 2013. ROBIN JONES

BELOW: The one-time rival stations Birmingham New Street and Snow Hill were never connected to each other by rail in the days of steam, but that could change when the Midland Metro is extended into the city centre streets, as depicted in this artist's impression. New Street has again been rebuilt following its soulless remodelling in the Sixties. CENTRO

It opened on May 31, 1999, and out of its 23 tram stops, 11 broadly match former railway stations. The tram stops are unstaffed raised platforms with two open-fronted shelters equipped with seats and a digital display of services, closed circuit television, and an intercom linked to the Metro Centre control room.

The Metro Centre, stabling point and depot is located near the Wednesbury, Great Western Street tram stop, on land previously occupied by railway sidings.

At Snow Hill, which became a rail-tram interchange station, Platform 4 was taken out of use to make space for the tram. Two stations, Jewellery Quarter and The Hawthorns, on the length of the Midland Metro which runs alongside the Snow Hill to Worcester line, are also interchange stations.

At the northern end of Line 1, the trams leave the railway trackbed at Priestfield to run along Bilston Road to the St Georges terminus in Bilston Street, Wolverhampton city centre, a few minutes' walk from the bus and railway stations. An initial proposal to run into the old GWR Wolverhampton Low Level station was not proceeded with.

There is a fleet of 16 AnsaldoBreda T69 articulated two-section trams, built in Caserta, Italy. The trams, which run at eight minute intervals during daytime on Mondays to Fridays take 35 minutes to complete the route.

How far has Beeching really been proved wrong?

Around five million passengers a year use the tramway, and there has been overcrowding at peak times. That in itself proves a public demand, and no doubt it had succeeded in reducing car usage, but the Midland Metro has not been a soaraway success, and it does not pay its way. When the plans were being drawn up, estimates for usage varied between 14 and 20 million passengers a year.

Conventional trains running between Birmingham and Wolverhampton are still quicker. In January 2013, the adult single bus fare from Birmingham to Wolverhampton was £2 compared with £3.60 by Midland Metro tram.

Critics have said that the tram is all but 'invisible' at Snow Hill, being reached via a long flight of steps on a cordoned-off platform, and does not have the visible city centre presence originally aimed for.

When Line 1 opened, it was run by Altram, and it soon became clear that receipts did not cover operating costs. In February 2003, *The Times* reported that the Metro's auditors had refused to sign off its accounts as a going concern.

Ansaldo and Laing pulled out of the Midland Metro, leaving its operation down to Travel Midland Metro, with the line's losses largely covered by cross-subsidies from other parts of National Express's business.

The Commission for Integrated Transport produced figures which showed that in 2004 it cost £3.79 per kilometre to run light rail trams, as opposed to just 94p for buses. Beeching-era calculations still evidently held good.

It also said that the fares needed for the Midland Metro to cover its costs was double that of Manchester Metrolink, London Tramlink and the Tyne and Wear Metro.

However, such figures do not take into account that several of the planned branch lines have yet to be built. If or when they are, they may well act as feeders to Line 1, raising usage and income. Line 1 would likely also reciprocate.

Permission was granted in July 2005 for an extension into Birmingham city centre, taking Line 1 through city streets into the heart of the main shopping centre. The tramline's existing Snow Hill terminus will be replaced by a fourth new stop near to St Chad's Circus, and the Metro platform returned to traditional rail use.

On February 16, 2012, the Government approved the extension, along with a new fleet of trams and a new depot at Wednesbury. The extension is expected to open in March 2015.

An extension from the present Wolverhampton terminus running directly to the bus and railway stations is also being progressed by Centro.

Other long-planned extensions include a line from Wednesbury over the formation of the disused South Staffordshire Railway, which ran from Lichfield via Walsall to Dudley and Stourbridge, and of which very little remains in freight use today. Network Rail also has plans to reopen much of the route for freight, so a scheme whereby conventional rail and tramlines can exist side by side is needed.

In March 2011, the business plan for the reopening of the South Staffordshire Line between Walsall and Stourbridge for the Midland Metro was submitted to Network Rail. Centro said the line, which would link to the giant Merry Hill shopping centre at Brierley Hill, would be built in stages, with the first section running from Wednesbury to Dudley, which, with a population of 194,000, has long been the biggest town in Britain without a railway station, the nearest being Dudley Port on the Birmingham to Wolverhampton line.

No final decision has been made, and experts have said that the ideas of trams sharing a freight line is unrealistic.

A light rail line or alternative rapid transit system from the city centre to the overspill estate of Chelmsley Wood and on southwards to Birmingham International Airport, has also been mooted.

The revival of the old GWR main line as light rail has brought many benefits to the West Midlands, but it is clear than its full potential has yet to be unlocked, and it may well be the case that it destined is to be viewed indefinitely as an environmental enterprise, relying on subsidies which are justified by providing an alternative to road traffic congestion and worsening air pollution from car exhausts.

There is a long way to go before the Metro becomes self-supporting, but few will nonetheless disagree that the project has been worthwhile. We have come a long way in the half century since Beeching closures were approved on purely economic grounds, but there again, who back then foresaw the day when Birmingham would follow London with road traffic grinding to a halt?

Might it have been more effective to have relaid the route as a conventional railway, and simply add more halts and use lightweight tram-type railcars?

Either way, Snow Hill has risen from the grave, and will continue to play an essential part in the transport network of the West Midlands and indeed that of Britain.

ABOVE: The ancient and the modern side by side: Tyseley-based GWR 4-6-0 No. 5043 *Earl of Mount Edgcumbe* heads Vintage Trains' 'Whistling Ghost' special from Tyseley to Minehead via Worcester past St Paul's tram stop on May 25, 2013. ANDREW EDKINS

BELOW: The modern Snow Hill station is now a hub of local services for the West Midlands region. ROBIN JONES

ABOVE: LNWR G2 'Duck Eight' 0-8-0 No. 49443 on a short freight working at Hednesford on April 20, 1960. Built at Crewe in May 1922, this locomotive was withdrawn from 4A Bletchley shed on October 31, 1961, and cut up at Crewe a year later. The liberal coating of grime was typical of steam engines in the early Sixties when emphasis was switched to their diesel replacements. COLOUR-RAIL

Chase-ing
freight line survivors

A Class 104 two-car DMU arrives at Chilvers Coton with a Leamington to Nuneaton service on May 12, 1964. There are currently no plans to reopen this station which served a Nuneaton suburb. MICHAEL MENSING

The easiest of all Beeching cuts to reverse are in theory those where the track is not only still intact but being used for freight on a daily basis.

I say 'in theory', because pro-rail campaigners have traditionally met with stubborn resistance from uninterested local councils and the railway authorities themselves.

In most cases, it has taken several years to prove that there is a case for a feasibility study as a preliminary step, let alone to physically start work on any revival.

Two classic cases of hugely successful reopenings of surviving freight-only routes to passenger trains are to be found in the West Midlands.

One is the Chase Line, which runs from Walsall via Cannock and Hednesford to Rugeley Trent Valley. The other is the Walsall via Cannock's Nuneaton to Leamington Spa line.

The section of the Chase Line between Walsall and Cannock was built by the South Staffordshire Railway and opened in 1858, increasing passenger and coal traffic to Walsall

ABOVE: LMS Stanier 2-6-2T No. 40122 at Kenilworth with a local passenger train in 1958. This 1935-built locomotive was withdrawn from 7A Llandudno Junction shed in June 1962 and scrapped at Cashmores in Great Bridge in May 1963. COLOUR-RAIL

and the Black Country. The section between Cannock and Rugeley was opened by the Cannock Mineral Railway in 1859.

In 1861, the London & North Western Railway took over the route and widened Walsall station to accommodate passing lines through the centre for mineral and freight trains, leaving two loops for passenger trains.

Walsall to Rugeley Trent Valley was a classic Beeching cut, closing to passengers on January 18, 1965.

The line, however, was retained for mineral traffic serving the power station at Rugeley and local collieries.

Bloxwich station, the first stop north of Walsall, reopened for a special train on May 29, 1966, taking 600 members of the Bloxwich Excelsior Club and Institute and their children to Blackpool for a day's outing, British Railways made no charge for the use of the station, which nonetheless was subsequently demolished.

Walsall station remained opened, but suffered from losing passenger services on its northern routes, the one to Rugeley, the other to Lichfield, which has now for many years also been the subject of calls for reinstatement.

Up to the Second World War, Walsall station was the focal point of the saddlery town's trade, travel and commerce. However, the rise of the motor car saw its huge local importance dwindle until the Beeching Axe all but helped finish the job. By 1977, it was left with just an hourly service to Birmingham.

The historic station was demolished in 1978, to be replaced by a Marks & Spencer and the Saddlers Centre shopping mall. What was left was a modern utilitarian concrete passenger halt, a far cry from the scenario in 1900 when at its height, the station handled 1000 train movements per day and employed more than 200 guards, porters, shunters, clerks and officials.

The return to Rugeley

In the late Sixties, as traffic congestion worsened on roads around Walsall, calls for the Rugeley line to be brought back into passenger use intensified.

Cannock District Council began talks with British Rail over the issue in 1970.

On March 28, 1979, Cannock MP Gwilym Roberts tabled a question in the House of Commons, asking the secretary of state for transport what further study he had given to the need to reopen the Walsall to Rugeley railway line. He was told that studies on the costing of services on this and other lines which British Rail was undertaking for the Association of County Councils were awaited.

In 1984, British Rail concluded a £20,000 feasibility study which found that it was practical to reintroduce passenger services.

Lobby group Railfuture Midlands and others fought a campaign for several years to restore passenger services.

The battle was half won on April 8, 1989, when Hednesford station reopened. The surviving southbound platform of the old station was renewed as the terminus of a trial hourly service from Walsall, with intermediate stations at Cannock and Landywood, which superseded the former Wyrley & Cheslyn Hay station that also closed in the Sixties.

RIGHT: An Ordnance Survey half-inch to the mile map from the 1920s showing the route from Nuneaton to Coventry and Leamington Spa. Today it seems all but inconceivable that passenger services could be withdrawn from a route serving so many major centres.

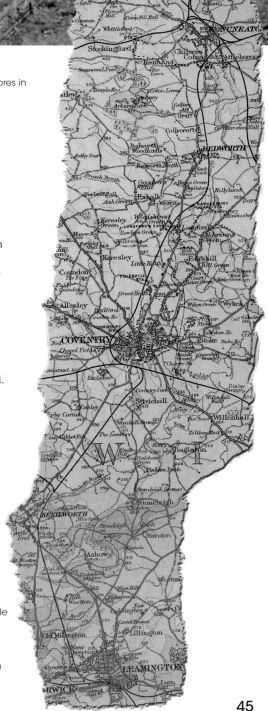

TOP: A Class 104 DMU calls at Kenilworth on January 18, 1965, the last day of passenger services on the route. COLOUR-RAIL

BELOW: Coal trains kept the line from Walsall to Rugeley open after the Beeching Axe fell on its passenger services, and they are still very much in evidence today. Freightliner Class 66 No. 66583 is seen passing Cannock. This train was emptied at Rugeley Power Station, then hauled to Bescot. KEVIN BOYD*

The services were run under the auspices of Staffordshire County Council, West Midlands Passenger Transport Executive, British Rail and Walsall Metropolitan Borough Council along with other local authorities along the route. A new station at Bloxwich was opened nine days later, but therein lies a story of its own.

British Rail did not receive planning permission to build the new station at Croxdene Avenue until after work had begun. The application for planning permission was late in submission.

British Rail later discovered that the platform it was building was not long enough for the revived services. Work to extend it was begun, but again without planning permission. Retrospective approval was, as expected, given.

Bloxwich North station opened on October 2, 1990, serving new housing on the northern edge of the town.

Initially, the station, originally known as Broad Lane, was just opened experimentally, but has remained in place since then.

The new Walsall to Hednesford service was an immediate success, vindicating the campaigners' belief that a local need indeed existed. The service immediately achieved 50% above break-even passenger levels, and led to renewed calls to extend it further north, to join the West Coast Main Line at Rugeley Trent Valley.

That happened in two stages. On June 2, 1997, a new twin-platform station at Rugeley Town was opened, the £1 million cost being met by Staffordshire County Council and Cannock Chase District Council. A new northbound platform was opened at Hednesford station.

The final stage of reopening took place on May 25, 1998, when passenger services were extended the short distance to Rugeley Trent Valley.

Using the route now being branded under the banner of the Chase Line – taking the name from Cannock Chase through which the northern section runs – trains from towns long disenfranchised from the rail network on Beeching recommendations were once again able to run straight into Birmingham city centre.

Central Trains managing director Mark Causebrook, enthusing over a 12% growth in rail passengers over the previous year, said: "We are riding on the crest of a wave with the opening of the Chase Line."

Monday to Saturday daytime, four trains each hour run from Birmingham New Street to Walsall. Two per hour call at all stations, the other two per hour call at Tame Bridge Parkway and Walsall, continuing to Rugeley Trent Valley with one train calling at all stations and the other missing out some of the stations between Walsall and Rugeley.

On Monday to Saturday evenings and all day Sunday there are two trains per hour (one stopping and one semi-fast) between Walsall and Birmingham and an hourly service to Rugeley Trent Valley.

Services on the electrified route between Birmingham and Walsall are provided by Class 323 electric multiple units.

At Walsall, passengers travelling on the non-electrified line to Rugeley change to Class 170 diesel multiple units. Typical journey times from Hednesford are 21 minutes to Walsall and 45 minutes to Birmingham New Street, infinitely faster than corresponding road transport.

Walsall station underwent a resurgence in the wake of the reopening of the line to Rugeley Trent Valley.

In 1995, major improvements were funded by CENTRO with financial assistance from Walsall City Challenge and the European Regional Development Fund.

The station concourse was remodelled and new waiting rooms built, with a glass fronted waiting area and a large new canopy and covering much of platforms one and two.

The resurrection of Walsall's railway services continued in the late 1990s and saw the extension of the Hednesford line through to Rugeley and then Stafford, as well as the reopening of the Walsall to Wolverhampton service in 1998.

A setback came in December 2010, when the Rugeley service was cut from half-hourly to hourly on weekdays due to lack of funding.

The future is electric

However, confidence in the future of the revived route is such that plans are afoot to electrify it, bringing it into line with the Walsall to Birmingham line.

Network Rail was scheduled to increase the speed of trains on the Chase line between Rugeley and Birmingham from 45-50mph to 70mph by spring 2014, but following a decision to electrify the route being announced by the Coalition government on July 16, 2012, the line speed improvements were being reviewed to bring them into line with electric trains. The speed improvements are now expected in December 2017.

The £36 million improvement scheme will also see the introduction of automatic ticket machines at stations.

A Network Rail spokesman said: "The planned electrification and line speed improvements on the Cannock line will provide a better service for passengers, with clean, modern electric trains and reduced journey times."

Electrification is set to see the introduction of new services to Birmingham International, Coventry, Liverpool Lime Street and maybe even Euston.

It has been estimated that the electrification will create over 1300 jobs in the area and generate a further

£113 million of gross value to the local economy, as well as bringing down the overall operating costs of the line.

It seems that a very different medicine to the one prescribed by the doctor half a century ago is now effectively beginning to work a miracle cure.

The story of another local rail revival, that of passenger services along the existing six-mile freight line from Walsall to Wolverhampton, did not experience a similarly happy ending.

Passengers wanting to travel the short distance to their western neighbour had to board a train at Walsall, travel to Birmingham New Street and then change to another to Wolverhampton.

That all changed on May 24, 1998, when in parallel with the advances made on the Rugeley line, a passenger service which had previously existed only between 1958-65 was introduced on the Walsall to Wolverhampton direct line. A journey which had previously taken an hour was cut to just 13 minutes, half the time taken by bus.

However, poor uptake saw the service withdrawn in 2008. Pro-rail campaigners blamed the irregular hourly service, an acute lack of publicity and the failure to open an intermediate station at Willenhall for its failure to

ABOVE: Bedworth in the steam era: on May 12, 1964, LMS 2-6-0 No. 42981 approaches the station with a permanent way train comprising Catfish wagons. MICHAEL MENSING

BELOW: Ancient and modern: Class 170 No. 170514 arrives at Hednesford station passing new signals which made the steam era signalbox in the background obsolete. TERRY CALLAGHAN*

attract sufficient passengers. They may well be right, but the exercise also highlights the fact that it is not enough simply to start running passenger services on a particular line: a clear need must be shown to exist.

I've no doubt that Dr Beeching would have wholeheartedly agreed in this respect.

Two lines to Coventry

A similar situation to Walsall to Rugeley Trent Valley existed with regard to the LNWR's route from Nuneaton to Leamington Spa via Bedworth, Coventry and Kenilworth.

The Coventry-Leamington line opened on December 1844, with stations at Kenilworth and Leamington, which was renamed Warwick Milverton in 1854 when the route from there to Rugby opened, with a new Avenue station in Leamington.

On September 2, 1850, the line from Nuneaton to Coventry opened with stations at Counden Road (Coundon Road from 1894), Foleshill, Longford & Exhall (closed 1949), Hawkesbury Lane, Bedworth, and Chilvers Coton.

A station at Daimler Halt opened on March 12, 1917. The complete route fell victim to the great axeman, closing to passengers on January 18, 1965.

Both halves of the route remained in use by freight. Nuneaton to Coventry was also an important diversionary route.

As part of the route infrastructure rationalisation which formed the final phase of the Beeching era cutbacks, the Coventry-Leamington line was singled over the weekend of December 9-10, 1972, with a loop provided at Kenilworth. The broad approach was that with the advancement of modern technology, and more sophisticated signalling systems, why keep two lines when one would suffice?

In parallel with the opening of the new Birmingham International station at Bickenhill, the Coventry to Leamington line reopened to passengers on May 2, 1977, with no intermediate stations, to cater for Cross Country express workings.

All passenger services on the line are operated by London Midland which runs an hourly service in each direction, provided by a Class 153 diesel multiple unit.

One big stumbling block to reversing Beeching cuts was the expensive need to reacquire statutory powers.

By the end of the Seventies, the desirability of reopening some closed stations or even complete routes to passengers was becoming increasingly widely recognised.

A big deterrent to the funding bodies was the threat that if a service was reinstated and merely proved Beeching right all along because it could not pay, it could not be rescinded again without going through the formal process – and then there was no guarantee that consent for it to be withdrawn would be given.

It was a no-win situation which discouraged rail revival. North Devon Conservative MP Antony Speller sponsored a Bill which sought to allow the immediate closure of such experimental reopenings. It was passed as the Transport Act 1962 (Amendment) Act 1981 and is often referred to as the Speller Act.

Its provisions are still applicable, although the legislation has been subsumed into other enactments.

Under the terms of the Act, British Rail Provincial came up with the idea of reintroducing a limited

number of local passenger journeys between Nuneaton and Coventry, and this happened on May 11, 1987.

A single 'bubble car' provided services between the two destinations, and was considered successful enough for the intermediate station of Bedworth to be reopened on May 16, 1988.

The service was suspended for almost a year during 2004-5. British Rail gave the excuse of lack of staff.

At present there is an hourly shuttle service between Coventry and Nuneaton, while the line is also used by through freight trains, and goods trains serving facilities on the route such as Bedworth Murco Oil Terminal and Prologis Park Industrial Estate.

On December 14, 2011, the UK Government announced an £18.8 million project to upgrade the line. New stations will be built at the Ricoh Arena – home of Coventry City FC until the club moved to Northampton Town in the summer of 2013 following a dispute with the arena's owners – and Nuneaton's Bermuda Park while the platforms at Bedworth will be lengthened, and services increased to half hourly.

In July 2012, the Government announced that the whole route between Nuneaton and Leamington will, like the Chase Line, also be electrified.

The project will form part of the electrification of the Nuneaton-Coventry-Leamington Spa-Oxford route as part of an 'electric spine' to the port of Southampton, delivering a high-capacity electric freight route. The hope is that it will entice companies to locate in the West Midlands while taking freight off the roads.

Caroline Spelman, Conservative MP for Meriden, said: "Like everyone in the West Midlands, I am delighted about this new rail investment that will bring jobs and increased business to Meriden and the West Midlands. This Government's landmark decision to invest in an electric spine from Southampton via Coventry will do much to

ABOVE: Class 350 No. 350265 calls at Rugeley Town station. PETER EATON*

attract businesses to Meriden and more capacity on the Leamington Spa-Coventry line is invaluable.

"I am also pleased that the Cannock Line will be electrified – it is a vital commuter line to and from Birmingham and will affect some constituents who travel beyond Birmingham.

"Thanks to the Government's announcement, Birmingham will have capacity for 3900 extra journeys – a remarkable increase that will boost growth in the West Midlands as a whole."

Kenilworth back on line

The townsfolk of Kenilworth, which today has a population of more than 24,000, are frustrated by the fact that it has a railway almost running through the middle, but no station. The singling of the line has led to a shortage of

capacity, and fears that stopping trains will serve to exacerbate the problem.

Nonetheless, a new station for the town was included in the 2008-2009 Warwickshire Local Transport Plan.

On July 21, 2009, it was announced that John Laing had won a 20 year contract to design, build, and operate the new station, due to open in 2013. Planning permission was granted on station construction to go ahead in the immediate future.

However, in February 2013, Warwickshire County Council lodged a bid for £5 million to the New Stations Fund which the Coalition Government launched the month before. The funding for a new station in Priory Road was approved in June 2013.

The total cost will be £11.3 million, with the remaining money coming from the county council.

Transport Secretary Patrick McLoughlin visited the Warwickshire town and announced the scheme had government backing.

He said: "Our support for Kenilworth station illustrates our commitment to working with community and national partners to meet local transport needs... with the biggest programme of rail investment ever."

The new station will include two 109 yard platforms capable of being used by four-carriage trains, with provision for these to be lengthened in the future.

In the wake of the announcement, Network Rail began carrying out work to integrate the plans for Kenilworth station with the electrification and schemes to increase capacity, planned for the line between 2014 and 2019.

LEFT: Coventry-bound London Midland Class 153 railcar No. 153325 in the platform at Nuneaton. IAN HALSEY

Chapter Seven

Settle & Carlisle:
Friends outside and within

LMS 'Black Fives' Nos. 44871 and 45407 south of Garsdale with the return working of the Railway Touring Company's 'The Waverley' from Manchester to Carlisle and back on January 28, 2012. DON BISHOP

I n the aftermath of the Beeching Report of 1963, there was widespread public anger followed by protests at individual line closures, but so many of these were in vain.

Thousands of people might object to the potential loss of their local services, but the powers-that-be had already made up their minds, or so it seemed.

However, there were cases where chance fell that one or two unlikely individuals made all the difference between a route closing and staying open.

As we saw in the case of the North Warwickshire Line, an eagle-eyed weekly newspaper accountant who broke an embargo on a British Rail closure notice advertisement sparked off a rapid train of events which saved what is now one of the busiest commuter routes in the West Midlands.

When British Rail announced plans to close the 73 mile Settle and Carlisle route in the 1980s, after the writing had been on the wall for it since the Beeching Report, there were again mass public protests, which many feared would be in vain.

Yet history records that it was a handful of individuals who made all the difference… and none more so than one of British Rail's own managers. Ron Cotton was the surprising but very welcome 'friend within'.

Britain's 'most beautiful railway'

It is without a doubt that the Midland Railway's Settle to Carlisle line offers some of the most stunning vistas to be seen from a railway carriage in Britain. It has been called Britain's most beautiful line, other contenders being Brunel's Dawlish sea wall route and the West Highland Line and its extension.

The poet John Keats wrote: "Beauty is truth, truth beauty, – that is all Ye know on earth, and all ye need to know." That concept, however, cut no ice with Beeching and his team, and the 1963 report

ABOVE: British Railway (BR) 4-6-0 steam locomotive, 1953-1958. A freight train crossing Sherriff Brow viaduct over the River Ribble on the Settle and Carlisle line in the Fifties. ERIC TREACY/NRM

ABOVE: LNER A4 Pacific No. 4498 *Sir Nigel Gresley* at Carlisle with the southbound 'Cumbrian Mountain Express' on August 26, 1981. BARRY LEWIS*

recommended that all passenger services should be withdrawn between Carlisle and Skipton.

One core plank of Beeching's strategies to make railways pay was to eliminate duplication of routes, and the Settle & Carlisle was, with much justification, in this concept seen as a poor second to the West Coast Main Line, which was being electrified.

Indeed, the origins of the Settle & Carlisle date back to the days when the Midland Railway was locked in competition with the London & North Western Railway for London to Scotland traffic, and was built as a rival and alternative route.

Plans for the Settle & Carlisle line were drawn up by the Midland Railway as the climax to a long-running dispute with the LNWR on access to Scotland.

The Midland trains ran to Scotland via the 'Little North Western' route to Ingleton and Lowgill, where it joined the Lancaster & Carlisle Railway, which was run by the LNWR.

The LNWR and Midland could not agree on sharing the use of Ingleton station, so two stations were built a mile apart. Eventually the LNWR gave ground and allowed the Midland to attach through carriages to LNWR trains at Ingleton, so passengers could continue their journey north without leaving the train.

Yet the LNWR persisted in petty awkwardness, attaching the Midland's through coaches to slow freight trains instead of fast passenger services.

The Midland accordingly decided to solve the problem once and for all by building its own route to Scotland, bypassing lines under LNWR control and the troublesome Ingleton connection and linking straight to the Caledonian Railway at Carlisle.

Surveying of the route began in 1865, Parliamentary approval for the line was gained the following year, and following a period of uncertainly during a financial crisis in Britain sparked by a banking failure, building work

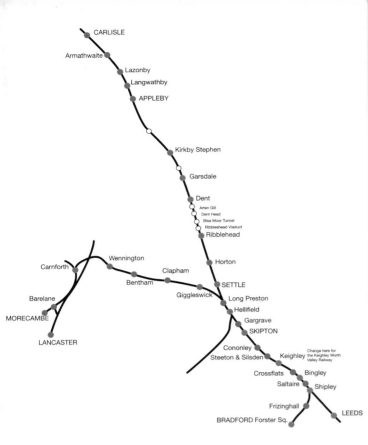

began in November 1869, with more than 6000 navvies toiling in the harsh Pennine weathers to hack it out of the stunning landscape by hand.

Engineered by Leicestershire man John Crossley, the Settle & Carlisle line needed 14 tunnels and 22 viaducts, and had its summit north of Garsdale at Ais Gill, 1169ft above sea level, the highest point reached by main line trains in England. The most famous of its structures is the 24 arch Ribblehead viaduct which stands 104ft high and 440 yards long. The swampy ground meant that the piers had to be sunk 25ft below the peat and set in concrete in order to provide a suitable foundation. There is also a 16 mile section of 1-in-100 known to enginemen as the 'Long Drag'.

To maintain speed, water troughs were laid between the tracks at Garsdale enabling steam engines to take water without losing speed.

The 73 mile line which took Midland services between Leeds and Carlisle cost 50% more to build than had been originally estimated, around £250 million by current values.

It opened for goods traffic in August 1875 and passenger trains in April 1876, after which the Midland started to take the lion's share of Glasgow-bound traffic, as it offered more daytime trains than the LNWR and more comfortable coaches, including Britain's first Pullmans.

Yet the Settle & Carlisle could never match the West Coast Main Line in speed, because of the route's steep gradients. The Midland's London to Glasgow route was also longer, and trains stopped many more times, to serve the big urban areas in the East Midlands and industrial north.

The downward spiral

The Settle & Carlisle was built as a duplicate line, and after nationalisation in 1948, it became increasingly recognised as such.

One of the drawbacks of the splitting of British Railways into regions meant the Midland route from London to Scotland fell under the control of different regions, whereas in the Big Four era, it had been simply part of the LMS. Accordingly, it became more difficult to schedule through services, giving a clear advantage to the West Coast Main line. Furthermore, mining subsidence affected speeds through the East Midlands and Yorkshire. Some of the smallest stations on the Settle & Carlisle line closed in the Fifties.

In 1962, the 'Thames-Clyde Express' travelling via the Settle & Carlisle route took nearly nine hours to reach Glasgow from London, compared with seven hours 20 minutes over the West Coast Main Line.

In Beeching's 1963 report, under the lengthy list of passenger services to be withdrawn, there was Carlisle-Skipton.

The writing was on the wall, even though the Beeching recommendation was not proceeded with. Behind the scenes, however, it was common knowledge in British Rail management circles that the route's days were numbered.

In the official report into an accident involving two Northbound Class 40-hauled goods trains, between Horton-in-Ribblesdale and Selside on October 30, 1968,

BELOW: The 1Z36 'Border City' railtour of March 24, 1984, headed by Class 40 diesels Nos. 40028 and 40086 seen during a photographic stop at Garsdale. The train started its journey at London and was one of many specials over the closure-threatened line. DEREK HOSKINS*

This view of a winter sunset at Ribblehead viaduct was runner-up in the Network Rail Lines in the Landscape award in the 2012 Take-a-View Landscape Photographer of the Year. GRAHAM RHOOSE

the inspector, Lt Col I K A McNaughton noted: "Even if the Settle and Carlisle line were planned to form part of the long term railway network of the country, it would still come fairly low in the priority list for installation of AWS; this route, however, is planned for closure within the next few years ..."

In 1968, 'The Waverley' from St Pancras to Edinburgh Waverley via Nottingham ended.

All stations on the Settle & Carlisle line apart from Settle and Appleby West were closed on May 4, 1970, with the withdrawal of the local Carlisle-Skipton service that Beeching had sought, while the passenger service was reduced to just two trains a day in each direction.

The 'Thames-Clyde Express' from London to Glasgow via Leicester was withdrawn in 1975, and the night sleepers from London to Glasgow over the Settle & Carlisle followed suit the year afterward.

A three-trains-daily service from Glasgow to Nottingham was withdrawn in May 1982.

There was a brief tourism resurgence in the mid-1970s. DalesRail, an initiative promoted by the Yorkshire Dales National Park Authority to encourage ramblers, began operating services to closed stations on the Settle & Carlisle during summer weekends in 1975.

Freight kept the Settle & Carlisle open, but British Rail was reluctant to invest in the line, and much of the infrastructure, including many of the viaducts and tunnels, deteriorated. Much freight was diverted on to the by-then electrified West Coast Main Line.

However, by the Eighties, the majestic line was handling only a handful of trains each day, and it was an unkept secret that British Rail now wanted to go one better than Beeching had recommended, and close the entire line.

In advance of any official announcement, the Friends of the Settle-Carlisle Line was

formed at a meeting in Settle Town Hall in 1981 to campaign against the closure even before it was announced.

It was in December 1983 that the long-awaited announcement came. British Rail was to close the line because of mounting losses, keeping just short stubs in place to serve industrial concerns.

Ironically, on the day British Rail announced its closure plans, the overhead wires on the West Coast Main Line blew down. The Settle-Carlisle line thus proved its worth as a diversionary route for InterCity trains, proving that duplicate lines still had their part to play despite Beeching's desire to eliminate them.

Friends of the Settle-Carlisle Line

One of the primary reasons was the huge cost of repairing and waterproofing Ribblehead Viaduct, stated as £6 million. However, it was later demonstrated that the true cost would be much lower.

Formal closure notices were duly posted at the Settle & Carlisle's remaining stations. Protestors banded together and formed a joint action committee, bringing together the Friends, the Railway Development Society (a national rail pressure group) and Transport 2000.

Backlash!

In the Fifties and Sixties, British Railways had managed to close a multitude of loss-making branches and cross-country routes in the face of local opposition.

However, the threat to the Settle & Carlisle was different. Not only was it a main line rather than a branch, but two decades on from Beeching, the public at large had learned how to challenge authority rather than do as they were told and accept the inevitable. Questioning the establishment was by the Eighties not necessarily seen as radical or revolutionary, but expected.

The protest against the closure of the Settle & Carlisle was not local, but nationwide, with more than 32,000 written objections. Local councils joined forces with the protestors, claiming that the route had been deliberately run down and it was an example of closure by stealth. Traffic had been diverted away from the route, the costs of repairs had been exaggerated and not enough had been done to promote its tourism value.

Just as banning a record all but guarantees its elevation to the top spot in the music charts, so the threat to the Settle & Carlisle boosted passenger numbers, which soared from 93,000 in 1983 to 450,000 by 1988, with many of those travelling thinking it was their last chance to travel over the line. British Rail appointed a project manager, Ron Cotton, to close the line.

However, history records to his great credit that he did anything but. Instead, he became instrumental in saving the route.

In 1983, when he was passenger manager for BR's Liverpool division, he was told to set in motion the process to close the line. He thought that the process would take just six months.

A conversion on the railroad to Damascus awaited Ron. Once placed in charge of proceedings, he felt that closure of the line was wrong.

ABOVE: LNER A3 Pacific
No. 60082 *Neil Gow* hauls a
passenger train across Ais
Gill viaduct in 1960.
ERIC TREACY/NRM

ABOVE: London solicitor
Edward Album thwarted
British Rail at every turn.
PETE SHAW/FOSCL

Rather than run it down still further, he decided to market the line and increase the number of trains. He could do this because part of his brief was also to maximise revenue.

In 1986, he reopened eight stations closed in 1970 – Horton-in-Ribblesdale, Ribblehead, Dent, Garsdale, Kirkby Stephen, Langwathby, Lazonby & Kirkoswald, and Armathwaite.

Yet, bizarrely, nobody in the higher echelons of British Rail challenged him, leading historians to wonder whether the national rail operator was secretly doing its best not to bow to political pressure to close the route.

Ron retired from a 39-year railway career in 1987, by which time the campaign to keep the line open had gathered considerable momentum. His involvement in challenging the closure edict from within has been crucial.

Years later, he told *Heritage Railway* magazine: "Right from the beginning I felt it was a wrong decision, and I decided to market the line and increase the number of trains. Also, when I arrived only two stations were still open – Settle and Appleby – and I calmly re-opened eight further stations.

"Amazingly, no one from BR queried what I was doing."

One of the objections received to the line's closure was, famously, from a dog.

Ruswarp, a border collie cross, travelled the line with his owner and co-founder of the Friends of the Settle-Carlisle Line, Graham Nuttall. He 'signed' the petition to save the line with his paw print.

Ruswarp's objection was allowed to stand and he appeared at the Transport Users Consultative Committee inquiry in Appleby, Skipton and Settle which opened on March 24, 1986.

Hearings by TUCCs into objections to closures were a standard part of the furniture of the Beeching era. They would present their recommendations to the Ministry of Transport, which made the final decision. The minister had the power to accept or reject their findings.

The Settle & Carlisle TUCC report found that closure of the line would cause extreme hardship. One case of hardship came from a Halifax Town football supporter who lived in Appleby. He told the TUCC that, should the line close, he would be unable to get to matches, and the club needed every supporter it could get. He was right, as Halifax town later ended up in non-league football.

In May 1987, English Heritage offered £1 million, then its biggest-ever grant, towards the repair of Ribblehead Viaduct. Local councils raised £500,000 to help save the line.

In 1988, an English Heritage report showed that British Rail's estimates for the repair of Ribblehead Viaduct were vastly overstated. Revenue from passenger journeys had by then increased to £1.7 million.

Nonetheless, that year, Paul Channon, the Transport Secretary in Margaret Thatcher's government, said he was "minded" to give consent to the closure.

However, another saviour was at hand.

ABOVE: Class 108 four-car DMU comprising cars Nos. E53632, E59385, E59246 and E53643 at Settle Junction on the Up main line forming the 3pm Carlisle to Leeds return charter (1Z31) on Saturday, April 28, 1984. DAVID INGHAM

ABOVE: View of the Settle and Carlisle line as seen through a locomotive cab window. The route provides a vital link in the harshest of weather. NETWORK RAIL

Enter Edward Album

In 1986, London solicitor Edward Album was recruited by the friends to help them fight the closure plans, and was appointed to the group's committee.

He became a lobbyist for the organisation, having regular contact with government ministers and civil servants, in a role which demanded the utmost in tact, diplomacy, determination, financial and legal acumen, and most of all a belief in the cause.

Ministers, MPs and celebrities were invited to travel on the line to see its potential for themselves.

Mark Rand, who later became the friends chairman, said: "There can be little doubt that, without the legal work done by Edward in the 1980s, in support of the unprecedented public campaign of opposition to closure, the Settle-Carlisle line would not now exist. He wrong-footed BR at every turn."

In April 1989, Michael Portillo, Minister of State for Public Transport, wrote to Edward telling him that British Rail had been refused permission to close the line.

On Tuesday, April 11, Channon announced to the House of Commons that he had changed his mind due to the increased traffic on the line.

The announcement was rapturously received far beyond the Dales.

However, Portillo, who later acquired fame for his

Great Railway Journeys TV series, added: "I look to the Friends of the Settle-Carlisle Line Association to co-operate vigorously in supporting and promoting the line, as you have promised."

The friends kept their promise, and are still very much active today.

The Settle & Carlisle Railway Trust was formed in 1990, through the initiative of the friends and with the assistance of the Department of Transport and local authorities.

Its first chairman was Dennis Vernon, and he was succeeded in 1999 by none other than Edward Album. In an astonishing coincidence, the two had been together at Aldershot in 1955 as officer cadets, but had not remained in touch.

Today, Edward remains as a trustee of the Settle & Carlisle Railway Trust, and as a friends committee member and their legal advisor.

Mark Rand added: "Ever since the line's reprieve in 1989, he has tirelessly supported the S&C through the work of the trust and the friends, despite his 'day job' as a busy London lawyer.

"If anyone can claim credit for the line's salvation and subsequent outstanding success, it is Edward Album."

BELOW: The letter from Minister of State for Transport Michael Portillo announcing that the Settle to Carlisle line had been saved. FOSCL

Modern-day success

Today's big debate over the Beeching closures is as much about hindsight as the decision-making processes of his day.

Who back in 1963 might have foreseen the widespread demise of the British manufacturing industry in the Eighties, and the huge social changes that it brought? Who in their right mind would have dared to say that within half a century, there would be no deep mines in South Wales? We could go on with infinite examples.

The question remains – just how far into the future can we reasonably be expected to predict?

The Settle & Carlisle would have its day again. Rail traffic in Britain ceased to decline two decades after Beeching's report, and due to congestion on the West Coast Main Line, bulk freight traffic began running over the Midland's alternative route.

Imported coal from the Hunterston deep water coal terminal in Scotland is carried over the Settle & Carlisle to power stations in Yorkshire, and gypsum is transported from Drax Power Station to Kirkby Thore. The line has become an important diversionary route during engineering works, but as it is not electrified, trains such as Pendolinos need to be hauled by a diesel locomotive along the Settle & Carlisle.

Major engineering work to upgrade the line to the standards required for such heavy freight traffic was financed, along with additional investment to reduce the length of signal sections.

Since 1989, much work has been done along the line in upgrading stations and facilities, the highlight being Ribblehead station which had stood derelict for many years, but is now an award-winning visitor centre.

In July 2009 work to stabilise a length of embankment near Kirkby Thore, eliminating a long-standing permanent speed restriction, was undertaken.

However, the Anglo-Scottish expresses did not return, and there still is no direct service from Yorkshire or the East Midlands to Glasgow over the line. Arriva Trains Northern began a twice daily Leeds–Glasgow Central service in 1999, calling at Settle, Appleby, Carlisle, Lockerbie and Motherwell, but it was withdrawn in 2003.

The regular passenger services are usually operated by Class 158 DMUs, although other types appear.

In May 2011 early morning services were reintroduced, with one train in each direction arriving in Leeds and Carlisle before 9am.

Barking commemoration

On April 11, 2009 a lifesize bronze sculpture of Ruswarp the dog by Joel Walker was unveiled on the platform of the refurbished Garsdale station.

The statue commemorates the efforts of him and his owner Graham Nuttall in helping to save the line.

In January 1990, 41-year-old Graham died while walking in the Welsh mountains with Ruswarp. He and Ruswarp had bought day return tickets from Burnley to Llandrindod Wells. The faithful dog, then aged 14, stayed by his master's body through bitter winter weather for 11 weeks until being found by a walker on April 7. He was so weak that he had to be carried off the mountain.

Ruswarp was cared for by a local vet, with fees paid by the RSPCA, which quickly decided to award Ruswarp its Animal Medallion and collar for "vigilance" and its Animal Plaque for "intelligence and courage".

He lived just long enough to attend Graham's funeral.

The £8000 cost of the statue, which has been placed on a plinth on the Up platform at Garsdale, Graham's favourite place and close to the line's 1169ft summit, was met by a public appeal.

Chosen to unveil the statue were none other than Ron Cotton, then 77, and Olive Clarke, who in the 1980s chaired one of the two public inquiries into the closure.

The ceremony also marked the exact 20th anniversary of the announcement that the line had been saved, and also included the official reopening of the station after a £250,000 restoration.

At the ceremony, Jo Kaye, Network Rail's route director for the North West, said: "Rather than being something of a Cinderella line, the Settle & Carlisle is now a major route for coal traffic from Scotland to power stations in Yorkshire and the Midlands, and has a regular and growing flow of passengers.

At the same time, Eric Martlew, Labour MP for Carlisle and a vice president of the friends, tabled a Parliamentary motion applauding those who saved the line. It read:

"That this House welcomes the 20th anniversary of the announcement that the Settle to Carlisle railway was to be saved; applauds the efforts of those who were instrumental in the campaign to save the line, including hon Members, local councils, and Friends of the Settle to Carlisle Railway; acknowledges that this was the last attempt by any government to close a major railway line; and regards the decision as the start of the renaissance of rail."

Tourists and railway enthusiasts now come from all over the world to admire and travel on the Settle and Carlisle line.

The future for the route

The friends and other campaign groups would now like to see regular through trains from Lancashire via Blackburn and Hellifield, as another big step to boosting passenger usage of the Settle & Carlisle line.

The friends group has looked at the demand for travel from Cumbria and the Pennines to Manchester and its airport. The group estimates that more than 50% of the population fly regularly from Manchester and almost all travel there by car. It seems that there is a business case for direct services to and from Lancashire.

However, the coal traffic which has thrived in recent years may not last, in view of environmental pressures to stop building new coal-fired power stations and reduce acid rain. In recent times it has been announced that Drax Power Station will be converted to burn biomass, and in July 2013, the first of a new series of biomass-carrying wagons was displayed at the National Railway Museum in York.

In April 2013, it was announced that Scottish Coal had gone into administration, with the loss of 590 jobs at mines in Ayrshire, Lanarkshire and Fife.

Of the two main freight operators on the Settle & Carlisle, one transports coal from opencast mines that belong to a different company and therefore will not be affected. The other, however, has been heavily dependent on Scottish Coal and has had to negotiate with the administrators. However, imported coal from the Hunterston terminal may make up any shortfall in opencast coal carried over the line. The Friends would also like to see stone traffic by rail from the quarries around Horton-in-Ribblesdale, eliminating heavy lorry movements on local roads and through Settle in particular.

ABOVE: The Northern Rail Settle-Carlisle service travels through the sublime splendour of Mallerstang in Cumbria. PEER LAWTHER*

ABOVE: In certain circumstances, not only could individual people make a big difference to whether a line stayed open or not, but in the case of the Settle and Carlisle route, a dog played its part too. Friends of the Settle-Carlisle line co-founder Graham Nuttall with his border collie Ruswarp and his famous pawprint on the petition to keep the line open. FOSCL

The group is backed here by the Yorkshire Dales National Park, which wants to see reduced lorry movements at the three quarries by 50% by 2015.

With regard to Dry Rigg and Arcow Quarries, now operated by a single company, a Lafarge Tarmac Joint Venture, it is proposed to install rail sidings in Arcow that would be used by both quarries. Hanson, which operates Horton Quarry, is in talks with the Friends about a similar move.

Ribblehead sidings, which are owned by Hanson, are being used for the transport of timber from several local forestry operations, producing several trains a week.

There are calls to speed up services on the West Coast Main Line. If such calls bear fruit, more container traffic may be diverted on to the Settle & Carlisle route.

Edward Album said: "I do feel pride at what I, and others, have achieved, especially when I look at the timetable for the line at Leeds station.

"It is amazing what has happened, particularly with the freight. We thought our job was done when it was saved and we could relax, but it hasn't worked out like that!"

Bitten by the bug

For some of the Settle & Carlisle campaigners, rail revival had become a way of life.

In the wake of the reprieve of the line in 1989, several of them formed a new group to reopen the Wensleydale route from Northallerton on the East Coast Main Line to Garsdale on the Settle & Carlisle.

This was by no means a Beeching closure: the 40 mile trans-Pennine route had lost its passenger services in 1954.

The westernmost section of the line between Hawes and Garsdale closed to all traffic in 1959. The middle between Redmire and Hawes was closed completely in 1964 and was lifted.

ABOVE: Weekend engineering work on the West Coast Main Line resulted in some unusual visitors to the Settle to Carlisle line on April 6, 2013. Dwarfed by the snow-topped Whernside, a southbound pair of Virgin Voyager units pass Ribblehead station in the early evening sunshine. The route may become increasingly vital as a diversionary route in future years. JULIEN KING

Over the remaining 22 mile eastern section, Dalesrail excursion trains ran between Redmire and York in the 1970s and occasional charter trains ran to Redmire.

With the exception of goods trains serving the quarry near Redmire, freight traffic on this surviving section ended in 1982. Goods trains to Redmire ceased in 1992.

Businesswoman Ruth Annison, a seasoned Settle & Carlisle campaigner, called the first public meeting in 1990 to explore the possibility of reopening the line for passenger traffic. At that meeting, the Wensleydale Railway Association was formed, with Ruth as its secretary for 16 years.

The association aim was to restore passenger services to the surviving part of the route and then to campaign for the reconstruction of the 18 mile 'missing link' to Garsdale.

In 2000, the association formed Wensleydale Railway plc. In turn it launched a share offer to raise funds for development and operation of the line, and more than £1.2 million was raised.

In 2003, the company acquired a 99 year lease from Network Rail for the 22 miles of track between Northallerton and Redmire. Passenger services began on July 4, 2003 over the 12 miles between Leeming Bar and Leyburn using DMUs. The Ministry of Defence then showed an interest in using the line between Northallerton and Redmire to transport

Classic Pennine limestone country scenery: LNER A4 No. 4464 *Bittern* passing through the pastures a mile before Kirkby Stephen station. ARG

ABOVE: J72 0-6-0T No. 69023 *Joem* heads a packed 11.30am Leeming Bar to Redmire service through the disused station on Wensley on July 21, 2012. This train typifies the last passenger services along the Wensleydale line which were withdrawn in 1954, seven years before Beeching was appointed. The saving of lines like this highlight the positive exploration of what can be done to restore services rather than the Sixties approach of compiling reasons as to why routes should be closed. MAURICE BURNS

armoured vehicles to and from Catterick Garrison. This plan went ahead with the MoD paying for repairs and restoration of the line and the installation of loading facilities at Redmire, and these military transport trains continue to this day. The MoD did not object to the volunteer-led group taking over the line.

In 2004, passenger services were extended by nearly five miles to Redmire and Bedale, Finghall and Redmire stations were reopened. In the years that followed, visiting steam locomotives enhanced the wider appeal of the railway. The railway now has the opening of an interchange station at Northallerton as a priority, so it can easily link in with main line services.

At the other end of the operational line, plans are being drawn up to relay track to the tourist magnet of Aysgarth Falls as a first step towards Hawes and beyond.

One day, if the revivalists managed to reach Garsdale, they may bring another influx of traffic to the first line that they successfully saved.

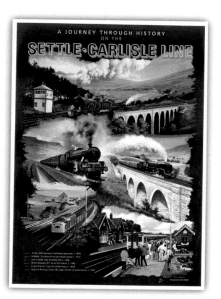

ABOVE: A poster produced for Regional Railways (North East) to promote rail services on the Settle-Carlisle line in 1992. Under the words, 'A Journey Through History', the poster shows a series of images of trains through the ages travelling on the route from 1876 to 1992. The artwork is by Pete Turpin. NRM

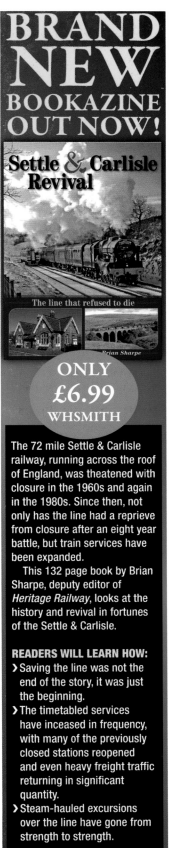

LMS Fairburn 2-6-4T No. 42218 at Worksop. Built at Derby Works and outshopped on January 22, 1946, this locomotive's last shed was 16C Kirkby in Ashfield. It was withdrawn on October 24, 1964 and cut up five weeks later. COLOUR-RAIL

The Robin Hood

Nottinghamshire's Robin Hood Line has been described as the most successful railway reopening in England, carrying more than a million passengers a year.

An important commuter service, used by more than 3500 people a day, the line also offers visitor access to several attractions in Nottinghamshire and Derbyshire.

The Nottingham to Worksop line, however, was never a single route in the steam era. It was reconstructed from two separate routes that had long been closed to passengers.

The first section from Nottingham to Newstead, a distance of just over 10 miles, opened on May 8, 1993, with Bulwell station following the year after.

The second phase was a five-mile extension to Mansfield Woodhouse, which opened on November 20, 1995. The Beeching cuts had left Mansfield, one of the largest towns in Britain (2011 population 99,600, and considered by some as a 'small city') without a station since 1964: from 1973 to 1995, the

nearby station at Alfreton was named Alfreton & Mansfield Parkway as a substitute.

Thankfully not demolished, Mansfield's station building was given Grade II listed building status and restored in 2001 for use by the Robin Hood Line.

The final 13 mile phase, an extension to Worksop via Shirebrook, which lost its passenger services in 1994, opened on May 24, 1998. Sunday services followed in December 2008.

Most of the line uses the Midland Railway route from Nottingham London Road to Worksop. After the closure of the line for passengers, the line was retained for freight use between Nottingham and the now-closed Newstead Colliery.

Beyond Worksop, the freight-only line followed the Midland route as far as Sutton-in-Ashfield, but between there and Kirkby-in-Ashfield, the line had been diverted to join the former Great Northern Railway route through the locality. This had been done to facilitate the sale by British Rail

of land in the centre of Kirkby-in-Ashfield, while retaining a route through the town.

North of Kirkby, the line rejoined the Midland route, where it remained is use as a freight line to Pye Bridge near Ironville.

When plans for the Robin Hood Line were drawn up, it was agreed to reduce costs by using extant track wherever possible. It was decided to keep with the GNR route through Kirkby to save having to repurchase land. However, after Kirkby, the new route was then designed to turn south-east via Kirkby South Junction on to the old Great Central Railway main line from Manchester to London, itself one of the biggest victims of the Beeching cuts.

However, there was a big stumbling block, the same as faced by the builders of the routes over a century before – the Robin Hood Hills at Annesley.

Both the Midland Railway and the Great Central Railway had been forced to bore tunnels to overcome this natural barrier, but after both of their routes were closed by British Rail, the tunnels were filled in.

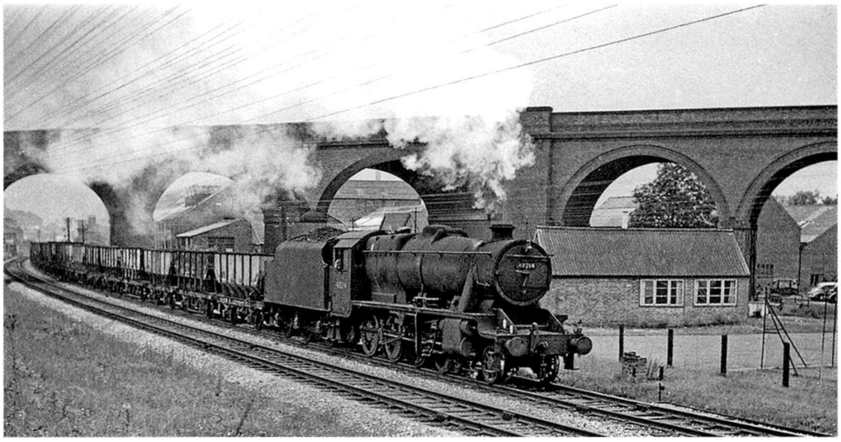

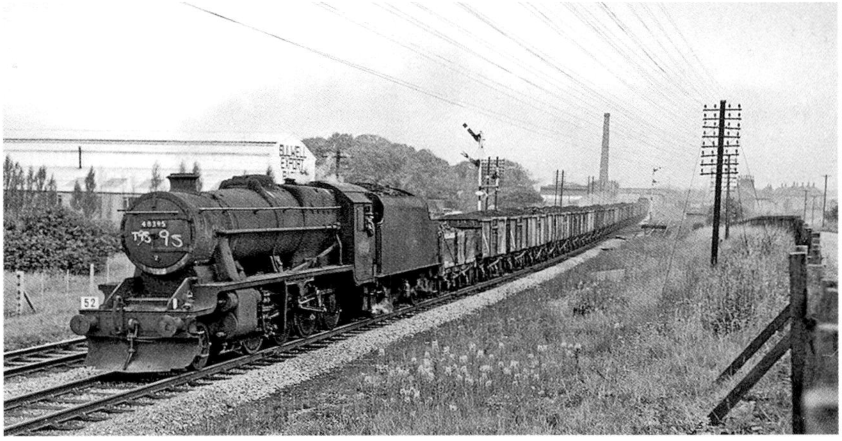

TOP: LMS Stanier 8F 2-8-0 No. 48214 passing under the Great Central main line viaduct north of Bulwell with a train of empty wagons on the Midland Railway's Nottingham-Mansfield-Worksop route, which is now the Robin Hood Line. The viaduct was demolished long ago. BEN BROOKSBANK*

ABOVE: Stanier 8F 2-8-0 No. 48395 – fitted with a snowplough even though it is midsummer – heads a loaded coal train near Bestwood Colliery sidings on the Nottingham-Mansfield-Worksop line, probably from Kirkby sidings, on July 12, 1963. BEN BROOKSBANK*

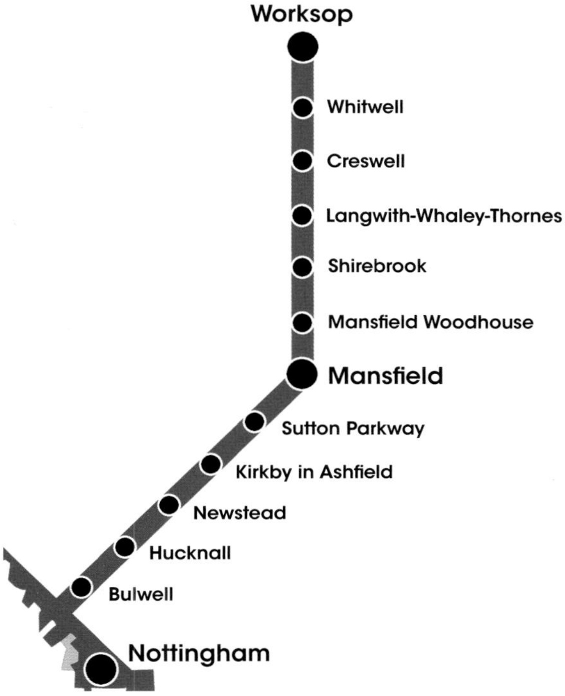

ABOVE: The route of today's Robin Hood Line, on which services are run by East Midlands Trains.

Line

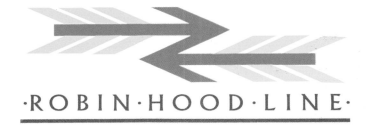

·ROBIN·HOOD·LINE·

It was decided to open up the Midland tunnel, because it was at a higher level than the Great Central one and shorter into the bargain, reducing costs.

The Great Central Railway's tunnel had been at a lower level than the Midland's and so was much longer. It was therefore much cheaper to re-excavate the Midland's tunnel, which was found to be in excellent condition.

Since the Robin Hood Line was opened, the double-track length between Bulwell and Hucknall has been singled to free up the formation for the Nottingham Express Transit tramway. Opening in March 2004, it follows the Robin Hood Line as far as Hucknall.

Today, the Robin Hood Line operates a Monday to Saturday service between 5.30am and 10.30pm. During the day, trains run at half hourly intervals between Nottingham and Mansfield Woodhouse, with one service an hour continuing to Worksop

Passenger services are operated by East Midlands Trains, part of the Stagecoach plc group. The line serves Bulwell, Hucknall, Newstead, Kirkby-in-Ashfield, Sutton-in-Ashfield, Mansfield, Mansfield Woodhouse, Shirebrook, Langwith, Nether Langwith and Whaley Thorns, Creswell, Whitwell and Worksop.

All Robin Hood Line trains carry ramps to allow easy access for standard wheelchairs.

A Sunday service was launched on December 7, 2008, with 10 trains running between Nottingham and Mansfield Woodhouse between 9.15am and 10.30pm, with four of them continuing to Worksop. This Sunday service was funded by Derbyshire and Nottinghamshire county councils.

However, due to a low uptake north of Mansfield Woodhouse, Nottinghamshire County Council reduced its funding. From May 22, 2011, a reduced Sunday service was run between Nottingham and Mansfield Woodhouse only.

An extension to the Robin Hood Line from Shirebrook station has been proposed.

To the north of the station, a freight line branches off. It was used for coal traffic from Thoresby Colliery at the western end to High Marnham power station via Warsop, Edwinstowe and Ollerton at the other.

This line was opened by the Lancashire, Derbyshire & East Coast Railway in March 1897.

It was marketed as the Dukeries Route because it passed through an area of great landed estates. Queen Victoria's son Edward, firstly as Prince of Wales and later

ABOVE: Stanier 2-6-4T No. 42629 pulls away from Mansfield on August 8, 1964. Built at Derby Works in September 1938, the engine was withdrawn from Kirkby-in-Ashfield on October 24, 1964 and scrapped four months later. COLOUR-RAIL

BELOW: A pair of East Midlands Trains Class 156 DMUs pass at Kirkby-in-Ashfield station. EAST MIDLAND TRAINS

as King Edward VII, used the line, often to attend race meetings such as the St Leger, with the Royal Train using Ollerton station.

Passing into LNER control at the Grouping of 1923, the line closed to local passenger traffic in 1955, six years before the appointment of Dr Beeching, but summer holiday excursions to and from the east coast continued to call at Ollerton until September 1964.

Since coal traffic ceased, the 10 mile line has remained open and fully maintained in use as the High Marnham Test Track, which accommodates Network Rail's Rail Innovation & Development Centre, previously known as the Rail Vehicle Development Centre. The test track is rated for speeds up to 75mph and passes on a bridge directly over the East Coast Main Line at the former Dukeries Junction interchange station.

Nottinghamshire County Council commissioned a feasibility study in 2009 to look at a plan to extend the hourly service between Nottingham and Mansfield Woodhouse to Ollerton, calling at Shirebrook, Warsop and Edwinstowe (serving the Sherwood Forest Center Parcs resort).

In August that year, Network Rail said that because the line would now be maintained, it might increase the likelihood of passenger services being restored in connection with the Robin Hood Line at a later date.

The local collieries have ceased to function, but the area has steadily grown as a visitor destination, while former mining villages and small towns like Ollerton have continued to grow. With the infrastructure being largely funded by the use of the line as the test track, there seems every reason to look forward to the day when these places come on line again.

ABOVE: The logo of the Robin Hood Line set into Bulwell station's platform brick paving. MATT BUCK*

TOP: Class 158 DMU No. 158864 at Mansfield, where the original station buildings have been brought back into use. ROBIN JONES

RIGHT: Class 156 DMU No. 156064 waits at Mansfield Woodhouse. EAST MIDLANDS TRAINS

LEFT: Trials of signalling system and on track machine performance at the site of the long-closed Tuxford station on the High Marnham Test Track. Robin Hood Line services could one day be extended over this route. NETWORK RAIL

Chapter Nine

The North Yorkshire Moors Railway: a preservation pinnacle

In 1951, volunteers took over the near-moribund Talyllyn Railway in central Wales under the leadership of transport historian Tom Rolt, creating Britain's first operational heritage line.

It was also the first in the world to be run by volunteers, and began a bandwagon which would continue to gather pace, attempting to reverse numerous branch line closures enacted before, during and after the Beeching era.

The idea was not new. In 1929, when Suffolk's legendary 3ft gauge Southwold Railway closed, there were moves by local people to run it themselves.

Two years after the Talyllyn volunteers ran their first fare-paying trains, the Ealing comedy The Titfield Thunderbolt starring Stanley Holloway was a box office hit. The story was about a group of villagers trying to keep their branch line operating after British Railways decided to close it.

There was considerable inspiration from the book Railway Adventure by Tom Rolt, published the year before, which related his experiences in saving the Talyllyn Railway.

Several scenes in the film, such as the emergency resupply of water to the locomotive by buckets from an adjacent stream, or passengers being asked to assist in pushing the carriages, were taken from the book.

The film itself inspired future railway revivalists, conveying the message that ordinary people could 'have a go' and save their local line when the grey men in suits in the Whitehall corridors of power decided it should close.

The Titfield Thunderbolt came out in 1953, eight years before Beeching was appointed as British Railways chairman.

Between 1953 and 1961, thousands of miles of lossmaking routes on the nationalised network were closed, at a rate of between 150

and 300 miles a year, as road transport increased by around 10% per annum. During his first two years in the job, before the Report on the Reshaping of British Railways was released in 1963, Beeching rubber-stamped closures which had been recommended by divisional managers, and which would have gone ahead had he never been appointed.

In some cases, passenger uptake on many of the winding rural routes that were closed in the Fifties were down to single figures. In others, numbers were moderate, but far from capable of balancing the books. It was not rocket science to come up with the idea that, in theory, buses and cars could do the job better and at a far lower cost to the taxpayer.

There would always be disenfranchised passengers who suffered genuine hardship, even if the majority of those who lost their train services were content to some extent to

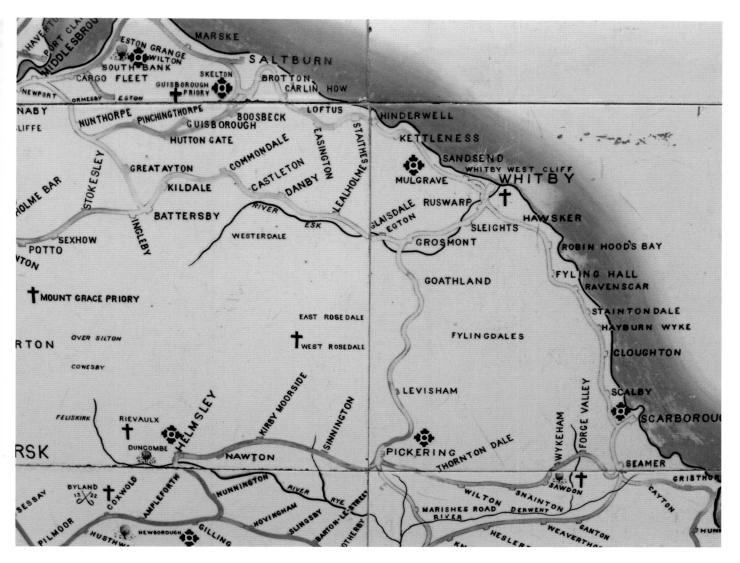

LEFT: LNER Pacific No. 60007 *Sir Nigel Gresley*, which is based on the North Yorkshire Moors Railway but runs specials on the main line, passes Darnholm with the 9.30am Grosmont to Pickering service. *Sir Nigel Gresley* is the holder of the postwar steam record speed of 112mph, gained on May 23, 1959, as it was descending Stoke Bank on the East Coast Main Line in Lincolnshire, where sister No. 4468 *Mallard* officially became the fastest steam locomotive of all time, hitting 126mph, on July 3, 1938. Most heritage railways including the NYMR are restricted to 25mph under the provisions of the Light Railways Act (1896) under which they are run. From this perspective they might not be considered as closure reversals in the absolute sense of the word. PHILIP BENHAM

ABOVE: The Whitby to Pickering route in the context of the railway network of North Yorkshire in the steam era, as depicted on one of the North Eastern railway's famous ceramic tile maps. ROBIN JONES

find alternatives. Those who could not were understandably among the most vocal protestors.

Inevitably, there would be those who would suggest that the closed line should be denationalised and handed over to the people to run, by and for the benefit of the local community, just as in The Titfield Thunderbolt.

Many such protest-cum-revivalist groups would start by aiming high, such as trying to retain an entire route. Such was the case with the Lewes-East Grinstead line, a small part of which was revived in 1960 as the Bluebell Railway.

It was the first example of a closed section of the standard gauge national network being taken over by revivalists, and in the decades that followed, many more would follow.

Only in a few cases would a revivalist group succeed in taking over and reopening a complete line. The Keighley & Worth Valley Railway was the first such example; the Dart Valley Railway's purchase of the Paignton-Kingswear line straight out of British Rail service was another.

In many cases, the intention from the outset was to restore timetabled round-the-year public services, but this rarely happened, and if it did so, did not last. Revivalists found out the hard way that despite the best intentions, there were reasons why lines had been closed. Even with enthusiasts and local people giving their labour free of charge, a 365-days-a-year operation was not possible, let alone viable.

What revivalists could do, however, was to tailor their line to run only the services that people wanted, and were prepared to pay to travel on.

No such option was open to British Railways. Many of the delightful seaside branch lines, which did a brisk trade in the summer months but carried few passengers once the holidaymakers had gone home, could not, as part of the national network, simply stop running during the winter.

Many such lines were closed because of the extremely high cost of storing vast fleets of coaching stock out of service for summer use during the rest of the year. Had such flexibility been possible, we might still be travelling to Lyme Regis or Ilfracombe in July and August by train.

A privately-owned heritage railway, however, remained unfettered by such restrictions. It could operate trains for identified markets, and when there were sufficient volunteers to man them. However, there would be no service by which local people could travel to work or go shopping whenever they chose.

A very different animal was thereby born. What was on offer was now a tourist attraction in its own right, not simply a means of getting from one place to another by the best form of public transport available.

A line may be reopened by revivalists, but as what? Not a regular public service, but as a living, linear museum, with a totally different business plan and structure.

There again, a popular steam railway might even carry more passengers during its comparatively short operating season than the British Railways passenger services did on the line before they were withdrawn.

However, it is highly questionable as to whether the railway is providing a public service as a people carrier, or running trains for their own sake.

This is by no means intended to be disparaging towards revivalists and preservationists. Heritage railways today form a sizeable slice of local tourist economies, creating or safeguarding thousands of jobs directly and indirectly.

However, only a few can say that they have run 'real' regular services, as opposed to tourist or enthusiast trains. Some have successfully run real freight trains, either as one-offs or as a series to serve an industrial concern next to the line. Others give local residents discounted tickets or free travel vouchers, which are much appreciated. Yet none come near to providing a full-blown all-year daily service of the type that British Railways and its predecessors did on the same route.

In short, the emulators of Titfield who saved their local branch ended up by and large in the tourist attraction camp as opposed to public transport market, despite their best original intentions.

Again, the message here is that there was often a good reason, if only by the standards of the day, why such lines closed.

On the other hand, if services could have been adapted to suit the specific needs of local people, rather than conforming to a daily timetable that the Act of Parliament which authorised the building of a particular line in the previous century had stipulated, with more room for manoeuvre and greater scope for initiative and

ABOVE: A large crowd of BR passengers got off the last train at Pickering – the 6.40pm from Whitby to Malton, extended to York on March 6, 1965.
MAURICE BURNS

BELOW: The closure notice on Pickering platform March 6, 1965. MAURICE BURNS

imagination, some closed lines might have been saved, albeit with a local transport subsidy.

This is not to say that heritage railways could never play a part in providing local public transport as opposed to tourist and enthusiast services.

The UK landscape has changed much since the years before, during and immediately after the Beeching era, and a station or branch line which might have been used by a handful of passengers a day might now be sitting next to a sizeable commuter housing development.

Provided an operating subsidy is forthcoming, there may well be scope for a heritage railway introducing peak-hour commuter trains, combined with an occasional shoppers services, alleviating the levels of traffic congestion on local roads that Beeching never saw in his day.

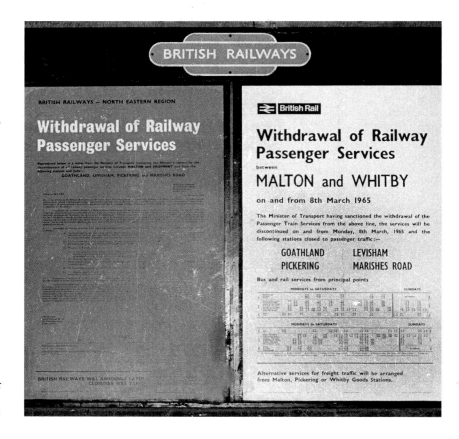

ABOVE: At a time when the railway preservation movement gained its impetus from enthusiasts bemoaning the loss of steam traction on the national network, the North Yorkshire Moors Railway's first motive power was none other than a 'despised' diesel in the form of British Rail AC Cars railbus No. 79978 on August 9, 1968. It was withdrawn in February that year, not even lasting in BR service until the end of steam, but ran in traffic on the NYMR until 1979, before being bought by Keighley & Worth Valley Railway members. Several early railway revival schemes, such as the Ffestiniog and Middleton railways, also began with diesel traction. JOHN BOYES/JW ARMSTRONG TRUST

The biggest heritage line of them all

The biggest of all heritage lines in Britain, in terms of passenger numbers, and possibly the world, is the North Yorkshire Moors Railway, which runs from Grosmont to Pickering, and also extends its services over Network Rail's Esk Valley line to reach Whitby.

The North Yorkshire Moors Railway began life in 1836 as the Whitby & Pickering Railway, designed in 1831 by *Rocket* designer George Stephenson as a late horse-drawn line.

In 1845, the railway was acquired by the York & North Midland Railway which re-engineered the line to allow the use of steam locomotives, in addition to the Beck Hole incline which was powered by a stationary engine, and built the permanent stations and other structures along the line which still remain today.

The company also added the line south from Pickering to Rillington Junction at Malton so that the line had a connection to York and London.

In 1854, the York & North Midland Railway became part of the North Eastern Railway, which in the early 1860s bypassed Beck Hole incline so that locomotives could use the entire route. The end result was the line we have today. The bypassed section of the original route is now the 3.5 mile Historic Rail Trail.

Beeching listed the route for closure in his 1963 report and accordingly, the final passenger service ran on March 6, 1965, although the line was used in June that year to stable the Royal Train for the Duke of Edinburgh's visit to the RAF Fylingdales early warning station. Freight ended in July 1966.

Local councils had fought hard but in vain to save both the Whitby-Pickering-Malton and Whitby-Scarborough lines, but were thrown breadcrumbs in the form of the Esk Valley Line to Battersby Junction and Middlesbrough. A winding route indeed, but better than no railway at all.

The demise of the Whitby to Pickering line was at first met with silence. However, local man Tom Salmon, who had wondered how to fight the closure plans as soon as Beeching announced them, set up a meeting at his home in Ruswarp in June 1967 to see if anything could be done to save it, as despite the haste elsewhere in ripping up tracks soon after the last trains had passed by, this line was still intact.

Several local railwaymen familiar with the line attended the meeting. They included retired BR driver Fred Stuart, a Whitby councillor who had fought the closure and even suggested using the rates to subsidise it.

In true Titfield fashion, he said: "If BR or the local authorities will not operate it, can we try?"

At a packed public meeting at Goathland on November 18, 1967, the North Yorkshire Moors Railway Preservation Society was established, with Fred as its first chairman and Tom as secretary.

While the wonderfully scenic coastal route from Whitby to Scarborough was by then being dismantled, British Rail agreed to hold off on the Malton route for six months while the society became established.

At first, it was agreed with British Rail to begin by reopening the Grosmont to Eller Beck section, with a new halt being provided near Fylingdales to provide access to the National Park.

The first item of rolling stock arrived on August 9, 1968, in the form of AC Cars diesel railbus No. 79978. Then came a first-class sleeping car to be used as volunteer accommodation. In November 1968, British Rail agreed to give the society complete access to the 18 miles of track using maintenance trolleys for carrying out essential repairs. Around the same time, a new company, the North Yorkshire Moors Railway Ltd, was formed.

The initial aim was to reopen the railway from Grosmont southwards through the spectacular glacial gorge in Newtondale, maybe rebuilding it to Pickering at a later date.

Early the following year, the British Railways Board approved the sale of the whole line to the

summit at Eller Beck, and the trackbed only to Pickering. May 19, 1969, saw a 10% deposit of £4250 paid.

On January 25, 1969, Hudswell Clarke 0-4-0ST *Mirvale* arrived on the line and steamed from Pickering to Grosmont, with British Rail permission, attracting huge crowds in the process. It was followed eight weeks later by Andrew Barclay 0-6-0ST *Salmon* and an 1898-built E Burrows and Sons 0-4-0 well tank owned by the Newcastle University Railway Society.

In the second half of 1969, British Rail singled the double track section of the line between Grosmont and Levisham. The move sparked a race against time to buy the remaining single track line through Newtondale.

North Riding County Council and the North York Moors National Park planning committee persuaded British Rail to hold off lifting the remaining track to Pickering.

However, by early 1970, it was apparent that there was insufficient money to buy the remaining track to Pickering. British Rail gave the society a deadline of August to come up with some money, or lifting would begin.

Mirvale and *Salmon* became the stars of an Easter 1970 steam gala which British Rail allowed to be held at Goathland, and it raised vital funds for the society.

Many heritage railways, including some of today's biggest, started out by running industrial locomotive types, wholly unauthentic to a main line setting, but which satisfied the general public's craving to see steam in the years following its demise on the main line in August 1968.

However, more appropriate locomotives for a former North Eastern Railway route were on the horizon.

The North Eastern Locomotive Preservation Group had been busy elsewhere preserving NER P3 J27 0-6-0 No. 2392 and T2 (Q6) 0-8-0 No. 63395, and the NYMR was a ready home. Also arriving in 1970 was Lambton, Hetton & Joicey Collieries 0-6-2T No. 29.

During a steam gala on June 27-29 that year, the Q6 and No. 29 hauled three-coach trains from Grosmont to Goathland, using volunteer BR steam drivers.

On March 27, 1971, the NYMR Preservation Society transformed itself into the North Yorkshire Moors Historical Railway Trust.

In early 1971, the British Railway Board agreed a price of £42,500 for the whole 18 miles of trackbed from Grosmont to High Mill, Pickering. The English Tourist Board offered a £30,000 grant towards the line purchase.

By now, membership had risen to around the 6000 mark, and a multitude of fundraising events were staged,

ABOVE: Fifties liveries to the fore: BR Standard 9F No. 92214 heads the 1.30pm Grosmont to Pickering service past Water Ark. PHILIP BENHAM

ABOVE: Large crowds gathered to watch *Mirvale* arrive at Goathland after its historic trip from Pickering on February 2, 1969. Many heritage lines began their public services running humble industrial steam locomotive types, before progressing to more glamorous main line types as more funds became available. JOHN BOYES/JW ARMSTRONG TRUST

from raffles and sponsored walks to collecting Green Shield stamps.

On July 23, 1971, a special train hauled by No. 29's sister engine No. 5 ran from Grosmont to Pickering carrying Alderman J Fletcher, chairman of North Riding of Yorkshire County Council, and his guests. It bore fruit big time, for on November 3, 1971, the council voted to negotiate with British Rail to buy the 12 mile line between Eller Beck and Pickering.

The idea was that the county council would buy the track and sell it to the NYMR over 20 years. The move would save the revivalists from having to re-lay the line in the future.

A fresh obstacle arose when Pickering Urban District Council considered allowing a supermarket to built on Pickering station. The Department of the Environment then saved the day by giving the station listed building status protection.

Royal reopening

Finally, the big day arrived, when the whole line would be reopened to the public – but as a heritage railway, not in its pre-closure format.

The first timetabled heritage services were run on Easter Sunday, April 22, 1973, with the official opening on May 1. The first public trains comprised a DMU hired from British Rail. The first public steam hauled train was hauled by No. 2392.

The Duchess of Kent arrived at Whitby by air to perform the official opening. She unveiled a plaque at the Angel Hotel where plans for Stephenson's original line were made in the 1830s, and then travelled by car to Grosmont to be greeted by a large crowd. There, she unveiled a commemorative plaque and was presented with a painting.

The duchess activated a signal to give the 'all clear' for the seven-coach royal reopening special train, double headed by No. 29 and No. 2392, to proceed.

Royal departure

At Pickering, a brass band led the duchess as she walked from the station to the Black Swan Hotel where she unveiled another plaque.

Running on the main line

Since then, the NYMR has gone from strength to strength, building up a sizeable fleet of main line steam locomotives and hiring others in from time to time.

Steam apart, one of the big draws for tourists is the upland scenery, which they can experience from the elevated heights of a train in remote areas not accessible by car. In this respect it is also a brilliant facility to national park walkers, who use the train to get straight into deepest moorland.

It is also a line for all seasons, not just the summer. Santa special services are run in the Christmas period, and winter moorland scenery adds greatly to their appeal.

An enormous publicity boost to the line's fortunes lasted several years when it was used for location filming of the Sixties TV police drama Heartbeat. Goathland station became

NORTH YORKSHIRE MOORS RAILWAY

THIS PLAQUE WAS UNVEILED BY
HER ROYAL HIGHNESS
THE DUCHESS OF KENT
ON TUESDAY MAY 1st 1973

TO MARK THE FORMAL RE-OPENING BY THE
NORTH YORK MOORS HISTORICAL RAILWAY TRUST OF THE
GROSMONT — PICKERING SECTION OF THE FORMER WHITBY AND
PICKERING RAILWAY.

TO GROSMONT, FROM WHITBY, RAN THE FIRST TRAIN ON
JUNE 8TH 1835, AND THE FIRST RAILWAY EXCURSION IN THE
WORLD ON AUGUST 7TH AND 8TH 1839.

THE WHITBY & PICKERING RAILWAY WAS OPENED OVER IT'S
WHOLE LENGTH ON MAY 26TH 1836. ALL TRAINS BEING HORSE-DRAWN
STEAM TRACTION CAME IN JUNE 1847 WHEN THE LINE WAS SOLD TO
THE YORK AND NORTH MIDLAND RAILWAY. THAT COMPANY BECAME PART
OF THE NORTH EASTERN RAILWAY IN 1854. WHICH IN TURN BECAME
PART OF THE LONDON AND NORTH EASTERN RAILWAY IN 1923. AND
BRITISH RAILWAYS IN 1948. THE GROSMONT — PICKERING SECTION WAS
CLOSED UNDER THE BEECHING PLAN ON MARCH 6TH 1965. THE FIRST
TRAIN OPERATED BY THE NORTH YORKSHIRE MOORS RAILWAY RAN
ON APRIL 22ND 1973.

THIS PLAQUE WAS GIVEN BY WHITBY RURAL DISTRICT COUNCIL

ABOVE: Norman Ash, driver of Lambton, Hetton & Joicey Colliery Railway 0-6-2T No. 29, talks to the Duchess of Kent at the official opening on May 1, 1973. J BOYES/JW ARMSTRONG TRUST

Aidensfield, and also doubled up as Hogsmeade in the Harry Potter films.

Other TV appearances include Casualty, Brideshead Revisited, All Creatures Great and Small, The Royal, Poirot and Sherlock Holmes.

Such nationwide exposure helped push the line's annual passenger numbers to around the 350,000 mark – a major heritage success story.

The NYMR has also extended regular services over Network Rail metals, with some of its locomotives passed for running over the Esk Valley line, either between Whitby and Grosmont, on special occasions, westwards to Battersby Junction and even Middlesbrough.

Many supporters were concerned about the extension of regular services into Whitby, fearing that the extra cost of running the trains and Network rail track access charges would not be covered by a rise in passenger numbers.

They were proved wrong. In 2005/6, the Carnforth-based West Coast Railway Company ran a pilot service from the heritage line to Whitby,

and in 2007, the NYMR became a train operating company in its own right to do the job under its own licence. So once again, a through journey over George Stephenson's route from Whitby to Pickering was possible.

From time to time, the missing 6½ miles from Pickering, where the original station roof has been replaced with the aid of Heritage Lottery Fund grant aid, to Rillington Junction, has been the subject of calls for reinstatement, finally reversing the last part of the Beeching closure.

Such a move would create a second through route to Whitby for public trains from the main York to Scarborough line, whole having the potential to bring in more visitors by rail to the NYMR.

However, the problems of extending the NYMR south of Pickering are compounded by the presence of a large road junction and supermarket immediately beyond the station, and houses built on the formation just north of Kirby.

ABOVE: LNER apple green and Gresley teak combination: visiting B1 4-6-0 No. 61306 *Mayflower* pictured near Goathland Summit while heading the 3.30pm Pickering to Grosmont service on May 6, 2013. PHILIP BENHAM

LEFT: Lambton tank No. 29 and B1 4-6-0 No. 61264 top and tail a service through typical moorland scenery, one of the big selling points of the North Yorkshire Moors Railway, which carries many walkers and ramblers to upland places which the car cannot access. NYMR

71

ABOVE: A4 Pacific No. 60007 *Sir Nigel Gresley*, in its striking early British Railways express passenger blue livery, departs the popular tourist destination of Goathland with the 12.30pm Grosmont to Pickering service on May 25, 2013. PHILIP BENHAM

Reinstating this missing link was adopted as a policy objective by the North Yorkshire County Council several years ago. The NYMR trust board supports the policy in principle, but would not undertake such reinstatement itself.

Extending NYMR services to Malton is seen as being of little gain, as the section between Pickering and Rillington Junction is a diametric contrast to the NYMR, comprising flat and featureless landscape largely unappealing to tourists.

The NYMR would support a separate company rebuilding the missing section but its officials have doubts about the impact of regular modern DMU

services being shared with the heritage steam services which bring in the crowds, and with them the vital income to keep the line running. Despite the huge annual fare-paying passenger numbers, the NYMR, unlike Network Rail, is still largely reliant on volunteers.

As much of the route was once double track, it might be possible to re-lay the second line for modern services to run through to Whitby.

However, as yet, no operator has come forward with firm plans to reinstate the 'lost' southern section.

NYMR general manager Philip Benham said: "The railway is a different animal to public transport on the main line, and we are not transport providers in

ABOVE: End of the line: BR Standard 4MT 4-6-0 No. 75029 simmers in the platform at Network Rail's Whitby station, now a regular and successful destination for North Yorkshire Moors Railway trains. ROBIN JONES

ABOVE: As if British Railways had never gone away: BR Standard 4MT 4-6-0 No. 75029 arrives at Pickering, where the historic trainshed roof has been restored, on February 21, 2013. PHILIP BENHAM

ABOVE: BR Standard 4MT 4-6-0 No. 75029 *The Green Knight* passes beneath the classic North Eastern Railway footbridge as it enters Pickering station with a 4.30pm service from Grosmont. PHILIP BENHAM

ABOVE: One of the North Yorkshire Moors Railway's biggest innovations since reopening has been running services on the adjoining Esk Valley Line from Middlesbrough, which was the only route into Whitby to survive the Beeching cuts. The subsidised branch now runs as a community rail partnership, and the extra revenue from the heritage operations – allowing NYMR trains to run regularly into Whitby, where a second platform is to be opened to accommodate even more of them – goes some way towards balancing the books, while again playing a major part in the tourist economy of the port. On May 4, 2013, LNER B1 4-6-0 No. 61264, masquerading as scrapped sister No. 61002, passes Lealholm on the Esk Valley line with the 2pm Whitby to Battersby service during the NYMR's successful 40th anniversary festival. PHILIP BENHAM

the strictest sense. We offer deals to local residents such as free travel on market days, but it is not taken up in huge numbers.

"We are a transport provider for visitors and walkers in the North Yorkshire Moors National Park, and we find that many people who want a day in Whitby take the train there as part of the experience."

North Yorkshire lost the regular public services of a line that according to official statistics struggled to break even when British Railways provided regular public services.

However, in the heritage era, it gained a major internationally-recognised multiple award-winning tourist magnet, that plays an integral part in the local

economy while also acting as a people mover at seasonal times. In this way, the achievements not just of the NYMR but of much of the UK preservation sector as a whole in reopening closed lines are somewhat reminiscent of Ariel's keynote song in Shakespeare's The Tempest:

Full fathom five thy father lies,
Of his bones are coral made;
Those are pearls that were his eyes:
Nothing of him that doth fade,
But doth suffer a sea-change
Into something rich and strange.

Chapter **Ten**

A welcome back in the Valleys!

One of the principal reasons for the construction of railway lines in Britain was the carriage of coal, which until recent times was the major source of industrial and domestic energy.

Almost every station in the country contained a goods yard to which coal supplies were delivered by pick-up goods services, and often a coal merchant was based next door.

The advent of alternative fuels for heating households such as electricity, gas and oil reduced demand to the point where coal deliveries by train were no longer viable. In some cases it had been receipts from freight which had propped up loss-making rural branch lines.

South Wales is Britain's only mountainous coal-producing region, and topographically is bisected by a series of valleys running broadly north to south.

Until around 1850 these valleys were lightly inhabited, but in the wake of 18th century development of iron smelting on the northern edge of The Valleys, mainly by English entrepreneurs, the South Wales coalfield was heavily exploited to produce steam coal and anthracite.

There were fewer than 1000 people in the Rhondda Valley in 1851, but the population had soared to 17,000 by 1870, 114,000 by 1901 and 153,000 by 1911.

Feeding the burgeoning national railway network was a mammoth task, and it required no less than a labyrinthine network of lines serving the South Wales coalfield to do so.

Independent railway companies like the Barry, Taff Vale, Vale of Glamorgan, Cardiff and Rhymney railways sprang up with the primary purpose of shipping coal from the mines to the ports of Cardiff, Newport, Swansea and Barry. The Great

Western and London & North Western railways competed in the area, the former gleefully taking over most of the smaller lines at the Grouping of 1923.

By 1913 Barry had eclipsed Cardiff to become the largest coal exporting port in the world, handling 4000 ships and 11 million tons of coal each year.

The 1950s saw the coalfield in marked decline as consumers turned to alternative fuels, with many industries using chiefly oil. Also, many Welsh coal mines were antiquated in comparison to other areas, and still relied heavily on manual labour rather than mechanisation.

From 15,000 miners in 1947, Rhondda was left with only one pit – Maerdy – producing coal in 1984.

In the aftermath of the miners' strike of 1984/85, the UK coal industry went into terminal decline. When Tower Colliery in the Cynon Valley – home to around 30% of the Welsh population – closed in 2008, it was the last deep coal mine in The Valleys.

In parallel with mine closures, unemployment in The Valleys has been among the highest in Britain. The families whose menfolk worked the mines for generations were still there, but the mines and jobs had gone.

The Valleys is suffering from several socio-economic problems. Educational attainment in The Valleys has been low, with a high proportion of people reporting limiting long-term health problems. A report compiled for the Welsh Assembly Government concluded that The Valleys is "a distressed area unique in Great Britain for the depth and concentration of its problems".

Job creation schemes have been under way for several decades.

However, one of the biggest saving graces of the post-prosperity Valleys was the key ingredient that made the coal industry tick – the railways that ferried the black stuff out.

Several of the branch lines were closed in the wake of the Beeching report, but have since been reopened to provide commuter transport into Cardiff, thereby widening the jobs market as well as boosting community transport. Today, a large number of people commute to the Welsh capital, particularly from Caerphilly, Torfaen and Rhondda Cynon Taf.

The same scene today: Trains on the reopened Ebbw Vale Line pass Aberbeeg Junction (there is no station at Aberbeeg) between Llanhilleth and Ebbw Vale Parkway stations. The mooted extension of the railway line to Abertillery would involve relaying the line from Aberbeeg. CHRIS SAMPSON*

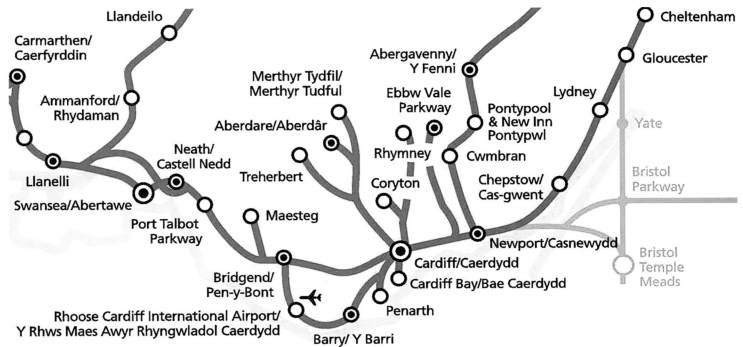

The Aberdare branch

The town of Aberdare in Rhondda Cynon Taf was first served by the Aberdare Railway Company's route from Abercynon and Cardiff in 1846. The company was later absorbed by the Taff Vale Railway and had a station at what later became known as Aberdare (Low Level).

Five years later, Aberdare High Level station on the Vale of Neath Railway line, between Neath and Pontypool Road, was opened. The two routes were later connected to each other at Gadlys Junction, and both companies eventually became part of the GWR.

Beeching hated doubling up of services, and also unprofitable branch lines, so for good measure, both were closed in 1964. The last train on the Vale of Neath line ran on June 13, and the curtain fell on the Taff Vale route on October 30.

The Vale of Neath line to the west of Aberdare was retained for traffic to and from Tower Colliery at Hirwaun, which was then served by the Taff Vale line. The latter route also served collieries and a coking plant further down the valley.

Goods traffic through Aberdare High Level ceased in 1965. The line fell into disuse, but was reopened in August 1973 to allow the trackbed of the Taff Vale route and its Aberdare station site to be used for road improvements.

All freight was then switched to the Vale of Neath line via a new connection between the two lines near Cwmbach and then on through the Aberdare High Level station to regain their former route at Gadlys Junction.

This new connection was taken over the River Cynon on a girder bridge that had previously been used to carry the defunct GWR Princes Risborough to Oxford branch across the A40 road at Wheatley.

No passengers, but the line was still very much open.

When the calls came to reinstate passenger trains, much of the infrastructure was already there.

Passenger services returned to Aberdare on October 3, 1988, when a new station next to the site of Aberdare High Level opened. It was funded by the former Mid Glamorgan County Council, and allowed commuters a direct link to Cardiff 22½ miles away.

ABOVE: An Abercynon branch train hauled by GWR pannier tank No. 6417 at Aberdare (Low Level) in 1954. This station was closed to passengers on March 16, 1964, along with the branch service. Services on the Vale of Neath line through Aberdare (High Level) ended in June 1964, but freight continued using that route. In October 1988, a passenger service was reinstated up the Cynon Valley from Aberynon, using the rebuilt Aberdare (High Level) station.
BEN BROOKSBANK*

RIGHT: The new Aberdare station shortly after reopening.
BEN BROOKSBANK*

The Aberdare branch runs from Abercynon on the Merthyr Line, and has intermediate stations at Penrhiwceiber, Mountain Ash, Fernhill and Cwmbach. In 2005, the Welsh Assembly Government provided grant aid to extend the stations at Abercynon, Penrhiwceiber, Fernhill, Cwmbach and Aberdare to four-car length to accommodate longer peak trains in a bid to relieve overcrowding, so popular had the revived services become. The Welsh Assembly also helped with train leasing and running costs.

The service from Aberdare is half hourly on Monday to Saturday to Barry Island via Cardiff Queen Street using Class 142, 143 and 150 DMUs. There is a two-hourly service to Barry Island.

The track still continues beyond Aberdare to Tower Colliery, where there has been talk of open-cast mining to extract around six million tons of anthracite to be shipped to Aberthaw power station.

In November 2009, the Welsh Assembly Government asked Network Rail to carry out a feasibility study on reopening the line to Hirwaun for passenger services. It was announced in March 2011 that the Welsh Assembly Government's 2011/12 capital programme would include the reopening of this northern section of the line.

We can therefore now look forward to the reversal of yet another Beeching cut.

ABOVE: Class 158 DMU No. 158831 in service on the Maesteg line. MATT BUCK*

LEFT: Arriva Trains Wales 150252 approaches the signalbox at Tondu, where the signaller is waiting to exchange line tokens. MATT BUCK*

ABOVE: Class 150 DMU No. 150208 arrives at Maesteg. MATT BUCK*

Return to Maesteg

A £3.3 million grant from the former Mid Glamorgan County Council and the European Development Fund turned an 8¾ mile freight-only line into a passenger-carrying railway once again.

The grant covered the cost of building six new stations on the Maesteg branch and providing three Class 143 DMUs which run from Cardiff via Bridgend to The Valleys town. The whole route today is branded as the Maesteg Line.

The South Wales Railway broad gauge main line from Chepstow to Swansea opened on June 18, 1850, later becoming part of the GWR. The Maesteg Line services use the section between Cardiff and Bridgend.

Running north from Bridgend was the standard gauge Llynfi & Ogmore Railway, an amalgamation of earlier lines formed on June 28, 1866. After threatening to build a

main line to rival that of the GWR, ending with the latter regauging its line all the way from Didcot, the Paddington empire took over the Llynfi & Ogmore on July 1, 1873.

The Llynfi & Ogmore line from Bridgend ran through Maesteg and on to Caerau. Beyond there, it passed through the Cymmer Tunnel into the Afan Valley and ended at Abergwynfi, where it also served a colliery.

In the wake of the Beeching closures, the Maesteg branch lost its passenger services in 1970, and Cymmer Tunnel was closed and sealed off.

During the late 1980s, local people began demanding the return of passenger services, especially as the line to Maesteg Washery remained in freight use.

The campaign paid big dividends – on September 28, 1992, a refurbished line was officially opened by Prince Richard, Duke of Gloucester. The reopening of the branch itself

included stations at Sarn, Tondu, Wildmill, Garth, Maesteg; and Maesteg (Ewenny Road) followed on October 26, a new station to the south of the town centre.

Elsewhere on the Maesteg Line, new stations were also opened in 1992 at Pontyclun and Pencoed; while on December 10, 2007, a new £4.3m station was provided on the main line between the pair, on the site of the original station axed by Beeching in 1964.

Arriva Trains Wales runs DMU services from Cheltenham Spa to Maesteg via Cardiff Central and Bridgend.

The railway north of Maesteg remained in situ until 2004, when it was lifted as part of the Maesteg Washery reclamation scheme. North of Llynfi North Junction, the formation, including Nantyffyllon and Caerau stations, is now part of major housing developments. Any extension of services north of Maesteg therefore seems impossible.

The Vale of Glamorgan Line

Closed by Beeching on June 13, 1964, the Barry to Bridgend route remained open for freight use.

Until June 12, 2005, that is, when passenger services over the 19 mile line were restored, two days after the line was officially opened by Welsh Assembly Government Minister for Economic Development and Transport Andrew Davies.

Another dazzling success story was Network Rail and the Welsh Assembly Government's decision to spend £17m on new stations at Llantwit Major and Rhoose, a reinstated bay platform at Bridgend and new signalling. The move was vindicated when 225,000 people used the services in the first year.

The line was opened by the Barry Railway in 1885, becoming part of the GWR in 1923. Freight included limestone from local quarries and cement from the works at Aberthaw and Rhoose. The opening of Aberthaw power station in February 1966 and the Ford engine plant at Bridgend in January 1980 helped keep the line open for goods traffic.

After the Barry to Bridgend services were withdrawn, passenger trains continued on the eastern part of the line from Cardiff to Barry and Barry Island.

However, the entire route was occasionally used as a diversionary route for passenger trains when the main line via Pontyclun was closed.

It did not go unnoticed that local circumstances had changed since Beeching made his closure recommendation, and that traffic on local roads had greatly intensified.

Railfuture Wales, a pressure group, produced Rails to the Vale, a booklet which claimed that a new daily passenger service over the line could now pay its way. With traffic to Cardiff International Airport increasing, local government transport consortium SWIFT saw the potential in reopening the line to passengers.

The project was promoted by the Vale of Glamorgan and Bridgend Borough Councils to the Welsh Assembly Government in August 1999, and work on upgrading began in June 2004.

A total of 3½ miles of new track was laid with a further 6½ miles upgraded.

Final planning permission for the new stations and interchanges at Rhoose, Cardiff International Airport and Llantwit Major was granted in 2004.

ABOVE: Porthkerry viaduct on the Vale of Glamorgan line. DR BLOFELD*

LEFT: The revived Llantwit Major station on the Vale of Glamorgan line. MICK LOBB*

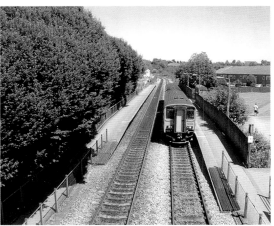

LEFT: Eastbrook railway station, near to Dinas Powys on the Vale of Glamorgan line. An Arriva Trains Wales service to Barry Island awaits departure. JOHN GRAYSON*

From October 2004, the line was closed daily between Bridgend and Aberthaw or Barry for the construction of the stations. At Bridgend, the Barry bay was relaid and a new platform face built.

Three contractors were involved – Mowlem for the track, Carillion for signals and telephones; and Galliford Try for civil engineering.

The Vale of Glamorgan Council was responsible for the construction of the interchanges at Rhoose, Cardiff International Airport and Llantwit Major.

The project cost £17m – a bargain price by today's standards for a new passenger-carrying route – with Network Rail spending the lion's share of £15m.

Welsh Assembly Government Minister for Economic Development and Transport Andrew Davies AM performed the official opening on June 10, 2005.

The Barry to Bridgend line opened two days later, when the summer timetable began.

Class 143 DMUs Nos. 143606/624 worked the first of the new public trains, the 8.40am Cardiff-Bridgend service and 9.45am return.

Arriva Trains Wales, the current operator, then ran several locomotive-hauled specials in conjunction with the Barry waterfront transport festival.

Ebbw Vale on line again

The branch to Ebbw Vale was opened by
Monmouthshire Railway and Canal Company on
December 21, 1850, with the GWR running passenger
services from Newport to the terminus.

The 18-mile line closed to passengers on April 30,
1962, under Beeching, but before he published his
report. However, the route survived in freight use,
serving the Corus steelworks in Ebbw Vale until it closed
in 2002.

Reopening the line to passenger trains was seriously
suggested in 1998, and four years later the Welsh
Assembly Government announced its backing for such a
scheme, as it would help the communities hit hard by
the loss of the steelworks.

The project to upgrade the line cost £30m, work
beginning in September 2006.

The money not only came from the Welsh Assembly
Government but also the European Union under an
Objective 1 grant and the Coalfields Regeneration fund.

The project was promoted by Blaenau Gwent council
and Caerphilly Council. It was the first time that a local
authority had taken responsibility for commissioning
and building a railway line.

A new terminus was provided at Ebbw Vale Parkway,
close to the site of the original Victoria station, with
intermediate stations at Llanhilleth, Newbridge,
Crosskeys, Risca & Pontymister, and Rogerstone.

Environmental issues delayed construction of
Llanhilleth and Crosskeys stations, after colonies of slow
worms, a protected species, were found near the tracks
and were moved to a safe place. Llanhilleth opened on
April 27, 2008, and Crosskeys on June 7, 2008.

Services began on February 6, 2008, run by Arriva
Trains Wales, using Class 150 DMUs. The first train
left Cardiff Central for Ebbw Vale Parkway at 6.35am,
while the first train to run in the opposite direction
left five minutes later, packed with dignitaries for the
official opening.

Welsh Assembly Deputy First Minister Ieuan Wyn
Jones opened the line along with Blaenau Gwent County
Borough Council's former Labour leader Hedley
McCarthy. The first train from Ebbw Vale Parkway was
waved off by local residents.

The Ebbw Vale branch revival was also a dazzling
success, and vindicated those who argue that lines which
were deemed uneconomic by Beeching in the early
1960s can once again become an essential part of a local
community in a world increasingly beset by traffic
congestion and delays.

In its first six months of 21st century passenger
operation, the line had carried around 250,000 passengers.

The figure of 44,000 passengers a month was double
the forecast, and above the 2012 target of 33,000.
Passenger journeys rose above 55,000 per month by
May 2009, and by October that year, more than one
million passenger journeys had been made on the line in
the 20 months since its opening, easily exceeding the
fourth-year target of 453,000.

Such were the loadings on Saturdays and at holiday
periods that extra carriages were needed to cope
with demand.

There is currently an hourly passenger service
between Ebbw Vale Parkway and Cardiff Central (but not
Newport) in midweek and a two-hourly service on
Sundays. The whole journey takes 57 minutes.

In 2009, the revived Ebbw Valley branch was named Welsh Project of the Year by the Royal Institute of Chartered Surveyors.

Judges said it made a significant contribution to the regeneration of the Ebbw Valley communities, vastly improving transport in the area and helping to support the local economy.

Blaenau Gwent now plans to upgrade an extra chord so that services can also run into Newport, which is currently avoided. Such a scheme would need some line redoubling and second platforms at Newbridge and Llanhilleth.

In May 2013, the Welsh Assembly Government revealed £11.5m would be made available for a new line and station taking the branch into Ebbw Vale town centre.

Finance minister Jane Hutt announced the project as part of a £76.5m funding package for housing, schools, flood protection and transport.

Blaenau Gwent AM Alun Davies said the announcement was "fantastic news" and strengthened the case for increasing the frequency of the service.

Electrification

Half a century on from the Beeching report, not only have the revived lines in The Valleys proved their worth in terms of serving local communities still reeling from the collapse of heavy industry, but also the Government is to electrify them all. What better endorsement of a reversal of Beeching policy can there be?

The aim is to have the whole Valley Lines and the Cardiff to Swansea main line electrified by 2020 as part of a £350m investment project, following on from the £1bn electrification of the Great Western Main line from London to Bristol and Cardiff.

Network Rail has described it as the biggest investment in Welsh railway infrastructure since the Victorian era.

Mark Langman, Network Rail route managing director for Wales, said: "Better links to London and

ABOVE: Class 150 DMU No.150230 at Ebbw Vale Parkway with a service to Cardiff Central.
ARRIVA TRAINS WALES

RIGHT: Rogerstone station on the revived Ebbw Vale line is built in the Afon Village housing development on the site of former sidings half a mile north of the original station. It has been linked to Newport town centre by bus, but plans are in hand to further upgrade the route so trains run into Newport instead of bypassing it.
ROBIN DRAYTON*

improved commuting opportunities around Wales, including to the new enterprise zones, will also help drive economic growth across the country."

The electrification of the Valleys Lines will build on the current £220m Cardiff area resignalling project, and will lead to faster, more frequent and more reliable journeys, with a 'metro'-style service for the Cardiff city region.

Passengers will benefit from faster train services between Swansea and London by 2018 when work to electrify the line will be completed.

The Department of Transport announced that the lines to be electrified are Cardiff Central to Cardiff Queen Street; Cardiff Queen Street to Aberdare; Cardiff Queen Street to Cardiff Bay; Cardiff Queen Street to Coryton; Newport to Ebbw Vale; Cardiff Central to Maesteg via Pontyclun, Bridgend; Abercynon to Merthyr Tydfil; Grangetown to Penarth; Cardiff Central to Danescourt via Radyr; Cardiff Queen Street to Rhymney; Pontypridd to Treherbert; Cardiff Central to Bridgend via Barry; Barry to Barry Island; and Bridgend to Swansea.

It will be one of the biggest investments in public transport in the region, with routes that Beeching and others did not want now playing an integral part in its future.

Chapter Eleven

The revivalists
who jumped the gun

Ticking all the boxes for closure as far as The Reshaping of British Railways was concerned was the 50 mile route from Cambridge to Marks Tey via Long Melford, also known as the Stour Valley Railway.

One of the longest west-to-east cross-country routes in East Anglia, it formed a backbone of a system including many smaller branch lines.

In the days before the car became king, it ferried goods to isolated communities, and as a diversionary route carried much holiday traffic in the summer months.

The first section, from Marks Tey to Sudbury, was opened on July 2, 1849, and was taken over by the Eastern Counties Railway on August 7, 1862.

The Great Eastern Railway, successor to the Eastern Counties, opened the line from Shelford on the London-Cambridge main line to Haverhill on June 1, 1865, extending it to Sudbury on August 9 that year.

When services started between Cambridge, Shelford and Haverhill, three trains each way ran on weekdays, and the service was extended to six passenger trains each way by the 1890s.

Coal traffic between Peterborough and Colchester and agricultural produce comprised most of the freight traffic.

After the First World War, cheaper road transport began making inroads into the line's customer base, a process which continued for decades until the doctor prescribed a mercy killing.

In 1954, an Indian summer for the line saw a regular through Saturdays express run in each direction between Leicester, Cambridge, Sudbury and Clacton, hauled by B17 Sandringham class 4-6-0s.

In a pre-Beeching bid to stem losses, steam haulage was replaced by diesel multiple units and railcars on January 1, 1959, making considerable savings.

The move briefly increased passenger numbers, but nonetheless many abandoned rail in favour of road, as did their counterparts in many areas across the country.

More severe pruning in the early Sixties saw conductor guards introduced to collect fares on board trains after all stations became unstaffed apart from Haverhill and Sudbury.

Passenger trains on the adjoining route from Long Melford to Bury St Edmunds ended on April 10, 1961, with Bures, Cavendish, Bartlow stations on the main route from Cambridge to Marks Tey closed to freight on December 28, 1964.

The publication of the Beeching Report immediately sent shock waves reverberating through rural communities on the Essex/Suffolk border served by the route.

The conductor trains and their cutting of operational overheads had done nothing to impress Beeching. His report said: "These suggestions ignore the high cost of the

ABOVE: The modern Sudbury station is a single-platform terminus on the edge of the town centre, managed by Greater Anglia, which provides all train services. This minimalist affair has a self-service ticket machine next to the platform entrance. Class 153 railcar No. 153313 has just arrived. OXYMAN*

Sudbury

Bures

Chappel & Wakes Colne

Marks Tey

ABOVE: The Gainsborough Line of today is the surviving stump of a 50 mile cross-country route which Dr Beeching recommended for closure.

OPPOSITE: Thompson B1 4-6-0 No. 61323 at Marks Tey, the end of the cross-country route from Cambridge via Sudbury, on May 20, 1961. Built by North British in 1948 to an LNER design, this locomotive was first allocated to 61 Kittybrewster (Aberdeen) shed. It was withdrawn from 31B March on November 25, 1963, and cut up at Doncaster the following February. Two class members, however, survived – No. 61306, now named *Mayflower*, and No. 61264.

route itself and that the rail cars are far more expensive than buses."

His recommendation flew in the face of comments made by a railway spokesman at area headquarters the previous August, who said: "I do not think anyone in the Sudbury or Stour Valley area has anything to worry about. Traffic in that area is still on the increase. Commuters from London are becoming more important".

The final years saw two trains a day run between Sudbury and Cambridge, four between Colchester and Cambridge and six between Marks Tey or Colchester and Sudbury, with the same number making return trips.

A partial victory

In April 1965, British Railways formally applied for permission to end passenger services from the whole route between Marks Tey and Cambridge.

The move understandably sparked local outrage and a lengthy campaign to persuade British Railways and the Government to change their minds.

The date for closure was set for March 6, 1967.

Local councils stepped up their talks with British Railways as the closure date loomed. A plan to save the line, reducing the losses to £26,000 by reducing services and running them only at peak periods, fell apart after British Railways challenged the figure, saying that a £52,000 subsidy would be nearer the mark.

Local authorities including Sudbury Borough Council, Clare and Halstead Rural Councils and Cambridge City, had no enthusiasm for the subsidy idea, and so the plan was shelved.

However, the minister of transport agreed that the Marks Tey to Sudbury easternmost section of the line should be retained, because of the fact that Sudbury was expanding and there was a potential growth in commuter traffic. It was a partial victory for the protestors.

All freight services on the Stour Valley line were withdrawn on October 31, 1966, and passenger services between Sudbury and Cambridge ended on March 6,

1967, the track being lifted by demolition contractor A King and Sons of Norwich in 1970.

However, the protesters scored a partial and major victory in managing to keep the section between Sudbury and Marks Tey open. Sadly, there was no reprieve for the Sudbury to Cambridge section.

The closure threat to the Marks Tey to Sudbury section did not go away, and British Rail, as by then the national railway had become known, made further closure attempts.

Finally, Ted Heath's government announced that the line would close in July 1974.

However, it was saved by events from afar.

The Yom Kippur war between Egypt and Israel and the resultant oil crisis frightened the government into believing that oil would run out, petrol rationing would be introduced by necessity, and that road transport would cease to run.

As a panic decision, the closure plan for the 12 mile route was hurriedly rescinded.

The threat of closure never returned.

As the Sudbury branch, the route is now a thriving commuter line. It is marketed as the Gainsborough line, after the great portrait and landscape painter Thomas Gainsborough (1727-1788) who was born in Sudbury.

Ahead of their time

An enthusiast-led group, the Stour Valley Railway Preservation Society, was formed on September 24, 1968, with the very overambitious aim of preserving all of the Sudbury to Shelford line. The aim was to follow the example set by the Bluebell, Keighley & Worth Valley and Dart Valley railways and succeed where local residents and councils had failed.

Their aims were quickly edited down to saving only the three miles from Sudbury to Long Melford.

The group failed here too, as it could not raise the money to buy the land.

Undeterred, in December 1969, the group established a headquarters at Chappel & Wakes Colne station on the

Class 153 railcar No. 153314 leaving Chappel & Wakes Colne station on the Sudbury branch. MATTHEW BLACK*

ABOVE: A Holden 2-4-0 tender engine sets off from Cavendish station in Great Eastern days with a five-coach train behind it. FOXEARTH HISTORICAL SOCIETY

ABOVE RIGHT: Sudbury kept its rail connection to London despite the best efforts of Beeching and others who followed after him, but that did not stop its station building, which dated back to 1865, from being demolished in 1991 to make way for the town's Kingfisher Leisure Centre. PAUL MILLER

BELOW: Long Melford signalbox, with Bernard Salter in charge. Long Melford was the Stour Valley Railway's junction for the line to Bury St Edmunds. FOXEARTH HISTORICAL SOCIETY

Marks Tey to Sudbury section which was still open. British Rail gave the group a lease on the redundant goods yard, goods shed, signalbox and station buildings, a site which by then was largely derelict.

It was widely believed that the Marks Tey to Sudbury route would soon fall victim to the post-Beeching axe, and had it not been for events in Sinai, this would have happened.

The group decided to bide its time and wait patiently in the wings until the Sudbury branch was closed, and then step in with better resources and take it over.

It was to be a wait in vain.

At the Chappel & Wakes Colne station goods yard, the first public steaming took place less than four months after the group moved in, but the only operational locomotive was a Hunslet 0-6-0 industrial saddle tank named *Gunby*.

It carried passengers in a contractor's weighing van over a third of a mile of relaid track. Other locomotives and stock followed, while the group set about restoring the buildings.

Preserved steam in action at the East Anglian Railway Museum's running line next to Chappel & Wakes Colne station, which along with the rest of the Sudbury branch, remains open. ROBIN JONES

Operations at the site would always be limited to the track in the goods yard and within the station limits alongside one platform.

The enthusiast group brought a redundant footbridge from Sudbury, purchased land on which to build an engine restoration shed and workshop, and rescued and re-erected the Grade I listed signalbox from Mistley on the Harwich branch, after buying it for just £5.

The society's limited company was successful in buying the whole site from British Rail at auction in 1987, after selling a locomotive to a group of members.

However, members realised that saving the Sudbury branch was by then well beyond their grasp, for one simple reason.

The society, which by then had built up a sizeable collection of rolling stock and artefacts changed direction, in 1986 reinventing its headquarters as the East Anglian Railway Museum.

It was three years later that the society's flagship locomotive, Great Eastern Railway N7 class 0-6-T No. 69621, the sole survivor of a type that had once been seen on many now-lost branch lines in Essex, returned to steam.

In 1991, the society obtained a Light Railway Order to allow the running of trains over its short line within the confines of the goods yard, and in 1999, staged major celebrations to mark the 150th anniversary of the opening of the Colchester, Sudbury, Stour Valley and Halstead Railway. The museum provided a re-enactment of the opening train with guests in period clothes and a brass band.

Today, the preservationists and the line they hoped to save exist side by side. However, if someone ever decides to axe the Sudbury branch, a safety net is ready and in place.

Meanwhile, in 1995, the Cambridge to Sudbury Rail Renewal Association was formed to campaign for the reinstatement of the line. Subsequent petitions in Cambridge, Haverhill, Clare, Long Melford and Sudbury were signed by more than 11,000 people, and a feasibility study indicated that nearly three out of four people questioned would use the route if it was reopened.

LEFT: Ancient and modern side by side: a Class 153 railcar running between Marks Tey and Sudbury on the Gainsborough Line passes a first generation diesel multiple unit at Chappel & Wakes Colne, home of the East Anglian Railway Museum. ROBIN JONES

LEFT: At Clare station, now the centre of the Clare Castle Country Park, a short length of rail runs into the goods shed, outside which the crane has been kept as another reminder of times past. The booking office and waiting room at Clare station have also survived. ROBIN JONES

ABOVE: The magnificent 32 arch 1136ft Chappel viaduct on the Sudbury branch was built between 1847-49. The first passenger train to Sudbury ran across it on July 2, 1849. It became a listed monument in 1967, and is believed to be the second largest brick-built structure in England. Thanks to the Yom Kippur war of 1974, it still carries trains today. R BELCHAM*

Chapter Twelve

Scotland
the brave!

I t seems that for decades, or at least since the mid-Eighties, politicians from parish councillors to prime ministers have espoused rail reopening as the great green future to solve transport issues across the country. We all know that Beeching was wrong; now we know all about global warming, so the more lines we open, the more people will leave their cars at home and the better the environment will be.

I have lost count of the times that I have heard such pre-election rhetoric only for deafening silence to fall once the candidate is elected. We've looked into it, it will cost too much, maybe at a future date we might consider it, maybe when the cost of petrol soars after yet another crisis in the Middle East and nobody can afford to run their cars any longer.

Blah blah blah, nothing gets done because there is suddenly every reason why not to spend the money, and slowly but surely more development encroaches on to the trackbed, another bypass provides another major obstacle, neighbours don't want noisy trains at the bottom of their gardens in marginal constituencies and so on. The ostriches queue to bury their heads in the sandpit while traffic congestion turns into gridlock.

Remember how the Labour opposition under Harold Wilson vowed to reverse all of the Beeching cuts if it was voted into power in 1964? Little seems to have changed in the intervening years in this respect, and too many green credentials aim for style rather than substance.

Most of the lines that have seen their stations reopened, the heritage sector apart, have been on routes that were relegated to freight only in the wake of the withdrawal of passenger services.

So who was prepared to take the bull by the horns and rebuild a railway in its entirety to serve the needs of the modern world?

Taking the lead

The answer lies in Scotland, a country which, had Dr Beeching's recommendations been carried out to the letter, would have been largely deprived of its country-wide rail network. Everything north and west of Inverness would have likely gone while the West Highland line and the Oban branch would almost certainly have not survived, leaving isolated communities historically poorly served by winding roads disenfranchised.

As it was, the Big Country lost the Waverley Route and also the 'Port Road' from Dumfries to Stranraer, a textbook Beeching closure of 1965, ferry trains instead being routed the longer way round by Ayr to avoid doubling up. Indeed, taking into account the loss-reducing mood of the

OPPOSITE: LNER K4 2-6-0 No. 61994 *The Great Marquess* heads the opening special at Alloa on May 19, 2008. IAN LOTHIAN

ABOVE: Class Deltic No. 55022 *Royal Scots Grey* departs from Stirling while returning to Alloa on an opening day special on May 19, 2008. IAN LOTHIAN

RIGHT: The Stirling to Alloa and Kincardine line being relaid. PAUL MCILROY*

FAR RIGHT: The new Alloa station under construction. IAN LOTHIAN

times, it is not inconceivable that Stranraer might at some stage have lost its railway altogether.

Setting the scene for rail reconstruction, as opposed to rail opening, was the 13 mile line between Stirling, Alloa and Kincardine, which competed with the Channel Tunnel Rail Link for becoming the first new addition to the national network in decades.

The project, which aimed to reduce congestion on the Forth Bridge by diverting trains such as those running from the coal terminals at Hunterston Deep Water Port to Longannet power station, as well as direct passenger link between Alloa and Kincardine in Glasgow via a junction with the rail network at Stirling, was promoted by a steering committee led by Clackmannanshire Council.

Original plans to revive the disused line for freight only were produced by Railtrack, the predecessor to Network Rail, in 1999.

The sole reason at that stage was the need to transport coal more efficiently between docks west of Glasgow and the power stations on the north shore of the Firth of Forth.

At that stage, coal trains had to use a circuitous route, heading eastwards south of the Firth and then turning north across the Forth Bridge. Weight restrictions on the bridge meant that the coal trains had to be split up, slowing down deliveries to the power stations.

The revived line provides a more direct, weight restriction free route north of the Forth.

Clackmannanshire Council decided to build on the revival scheme by adding passenger trains between Alloa and the existing rail network at Stirling, mindful of predictions of a 27% increase in road traffic between 2002 and 2020.

In 2001, the local authority was handed a £6.5 million grant from the Scottish Executive.

Railtrack began to be beset by the financial problems which led to its demise and replacement. In the meantime, the council took the lead on the revival scheme and formed a steering committee with other local authorities to obtain the necessary statutory powers through Parliament for the rebuilding of the line.

The committee included Fife and Stirling Councils, the Strategic Rail Authority, development agency

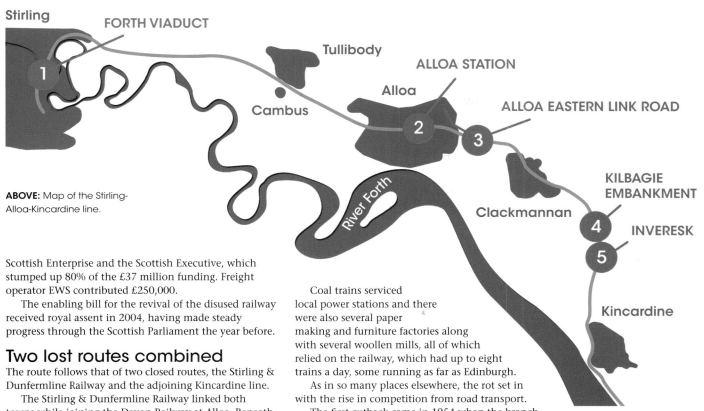

ABOVE: Map of the Stirling-Alloa-Kincardine line.

Scottish Enterprise and the Scottish Executive, which stumped up 80% of the £37 million funding. Freight operator EWS contributed £250,000.

The enabling bill for the revival of the disused railway received royal assent in 2004, having made steady progress through the Scottish Parliament the year before.

Two lost routes combined

The route follows that of two closed routes, the Stirling & Dunfermline Railway and the adjoining Kincardine line.

The Stirling & Dunfermline Railway linked both towns while joining the Devon Railway at Alloa. Beneath Clackmannanshire lay an extensive coalfield serving growing industry which was considered ripe for a railway.

The line was opened in stages between 1849-63, Alloa being reached from Dunfermline in 1850. Later acquired by the North British Railway, it became part of the LNER at the Grouping.

Coal trains serviced local power stations and there were also several paper making and furniture factories along with several woollen mills, all of which relied on the railway, which had up to eight trains a day, some running as far as Edinburgh.

As in so many places elsewhere, the rot set in with the rise in competition from road transport.

The first cutback came in 1954 when the branch to Alva closed. Passenger services on the line were withdrawn on Saturday, October 5, 1968, but freight soldiered on until the early 1980s. After the last goods train ran, the line west of Alloa remained in place.

The Kincardine Line linked Alloa and settlements along the north shore of the Firth of Forth.

BELOW: LNER A4 Pacific No. 60007 on a Scottish Railway Preservation Society railtour at Torryburn on April 24, 2011. IAN LOTHIAN

The section between Kincardine and Kincardine Junction on the Stirling and Dunfermline Railway was opened in 1893, with the line between Kincardine and Dunfermline opening in 1906.

Passenger services between Alloa and Dunfermline were axed as early as 1930, although the line stayed open for coal trains to Kincardine and Longannet power stations.

A fast road back

Rebuilding began in 2005, with tracklaying starting at the end of September 2006 and ending in March 2007.

Much of the project involved repairing neglected original structures and replacing the single-line track which has become overgrown since it closed in 1983. Indeed, parts of it, at Kilbagie and near the Blackgrange level crossing, had 'disappeared'. The ballast was also renewed, and waterproofing and soil reinforcing membranes were laid beneath it, along with new drainage.

At the eastern end of the new route, it was necessary to stabilise old mine workings; and near Alloa, work also involved constructing a short section of road, the Alloa eastern link, to take traffic away from two level crossings.

The recreated line also needed new signalling, level crossings and a new station at Alloa. A major bridge taking the railway over the A907 at Helensfield was completely renewed, with one new abutment built to allow the road to be widened. The steelwork of most of the bridges was painted maroon.

ABOVE: Class 170 diesel multiple unit No. 170475 faces towards Stirling at the new Alloa station. ROGER GRIFFITH

RIGHT: The Alloa branch was rebuilt to take coal trains away from the bottleneck of the Forth Bridge. ROBIN JONES

The project was completed at the end of March 2008, when driver training began on the line to familiarise drivers with the route.

The line reopened to the public with the first timetabled train to Glasgow on May 19, 2008, four days after a series of charter trains ran to mark the occasion.

The Scottish Railway Preservation Society, which has also restored the North British Railway's Bo'ness branch to Manuel Junction as an award-winning tourist attraction under the banner of the Bo'ness & Kinneil Railway, ran a special headed by LNER K4 2-6-0 No. 61994 *The Great Marquess* on four packed round trips, the first for VIPs and the rest for paying passengers. Class 55 Deltic No. 55022 *Royal Scots Grey* was used to haul the train back in the absence of run-round facilities at Alloa.

Later that month, much of the coal freight heading for Longannet was switched from the Edinburgh-Glasgow line via the Forth Bridge to the new railway, freeing up paths.

Ringing the changes

The new line is also single track, with passing loops at Cambus, to the west of Alloa, and Hilton, to the east. The passenger terminus at Alloa is equipped with a single platform. The new Alloa station lies to the east of its predecessor, due to the earlier construction of the town's leisure centre.

The original loop at Kincardine has been removed, and to obtain a better alignment, the junction accessing the

LEFT: The front of the modern Alloa station, which handled around 400,000 passengers in its first year of operation. ROGER GRIFFITH

BELOW: This view of Stirling (Shore Road) on August 28, 1948, eight months after Nationalisation, shows north British duo J77 0-6-0T No. 68351 and J35 0-6-0 No. 64520. The depot, which served the Alloa route, closed on September 16, 1957. BEN BROOKSBANK*

BR Britannia Pacific No. 70013 *Oliver Cromwell* hugs the northern shore of the Firth of Forth at Kincardine with a railtour. IAN LOTHIAN

former power station sidings has been moved to the east, with a new locomotive run-round facility in the yard.

Level crossings on the route were removed except in cases where alternative access would be difficult and costly.

It was predicted that the line would carry 155,000 passengers a year, but the trains were swamped due to public demand. After six months, this estimate was revised sharply upwards to 416,000.

The current service provides an hourly train to Stirling and Glasgow seven days a week, with an extra peak hour commuter service to Edinburgh six days a week. It takes between 12–14 minutes to reach Stirling.

The trains normally comprise Class 170 or 158 DMUs.

The Scottish Executive's faith in the scheme has been fully justified, and it remains as a pioneering blueprint as to just what can be achieved, arguably in the right place at the right time.

ABOVE: DB Schenker red-liveried Class 66 No. 66101 passes Alloa station on May 31, 2013 with a slightly late-running Longannet Power Station to Hunterston empty merry-go-round coal train. IAN LOTHIAN

ABOVE: There are two passing loops on the Alloa line. The first is at Cambus, west of Alloa and the other is Alloa Loop to the east of Alloa between Alloa and Kincardine. A Class 170 DMU is seen passing Cambus Loop on a Glasgow Queen Street-Alloa service on March 25, 2011. IAN LOTHIAN

It has been so successful that there is talk of extending passenger trains to Dunfermline and serving communities like Clackmannan, Kincardine, Culross, Valleyfield and Cairneyhill, or maybe extending services to the Rosyth ferry terminal.

Yet only as recently as 1999, thoughts on reviving the line centred exclusively on freight use. The initial vision did not foresee the huge social, economic and environmental benefits reopening the route to passengers would bring.

Many have condemned Beeching and those who hired him for the lack of long-term vision. Yet the

ABOVE: Great Western Railway 4-6-0 No. 5043 *Earl of Mount Edgcumbe* hauls 'The Caledonian' railtour at Kincardine.

LEFT: In May 2011 an extremely violent and unseasonal storm swept across Scotland bringing down tress, branches and masses of leaves. This caused track circuiting problems and for three days, a pair of Direct Rail Services Class 37s worked a Rail Head Treatment Train over the Alloa line. No. 37601 with No. 37611 on the rear are seen at Manor Powis on a Grangemouth-Grangemouth via Central Scotland lines working. IAN LOTHIAN

phenomenal success of the Alloa line has proved that there surely must exist scope for the revival of many other routes.

Clackmannanshire showed it did have the courage and conviction to proceed with the scheme, rather than relegating rail revival to cheap election promises. I'm sure that many readers will have their own views on lines which were declared redundant half a century ago and lifted, but whose time would now come again if only those who become elected to power to serve the wider community would allow it.

LEFT: The morning Freightliner merry-go-round coal train from Ravenstruther with Class 66 No. 66597 was running late and so passed No. 66035 with a Longannet-Hunterston empty merry-go-round train at Alloa Loop. IAN LOTHIAN

Chapter Thirteen

Swanage steam:
public transport in the 21st century

T he train was packed almost to standing room only. You had to walk through the five carriages to try to find a single seat.

It was hauled by steam yet, strangely, when it reached its destination you did not have the usual gathering of enthusiastic followers of all ages crowding around the locomotive, a typical heritage railway sight. Instead, the passengers walked past not giving a damn about what was hauling the train, but were simply bent on reaching their intended destination.

A London commuter train in the Fifties maybe? Far from it – this was the Swanage Railway in mid-August 2013.

Not only has the army of volunteers who over four decades rebuilt this London & South Western rail branch line from scratch effectively recreated a superb microcosm of the old Southern Railway and its successor the Southern Region down to find details, but has also restored its as-built purpose. It is carrying people from A to B and not just entertaining them as a modern-day nostalgia attraction.

For the Swanage Railway may be viewed as having come closer than most other heritage revival schemes to restoring genuine public transport services, where people use the train as a means of getting somewhere rather than a just a visitor attraction in itself.

Much of its success is down to the geography of the Isle of Purbeck. Similar to the chalk landscape of neighbour the Isle of Wight in so many ways, Purbeck is not an island in the conventional sense. It is bordered by the English Channel on two sides and Poole Harbour on the other, making it a type of giant broad promontory.

The spine road leading from Wareham to Swanage is the A351, and because all of the traffic leading into the seaside resort becomes funnelled on to it, the net result is

BELOW: The London & South Western Railway Swanage branch, as depicted on an Ordnance Survey one-inch map of 1937, when Corfe Castle was the sole intermediate station.

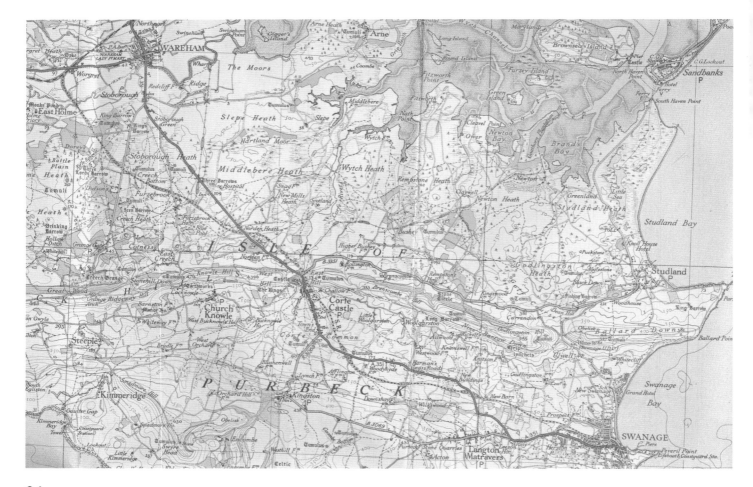

On May 2, 2009, history was made when Bulleid Battle of Britain Pacific No. 34067 *Tangmere* headed the *Wessex Venturer,* the first incoming steam-hauled railtour on to the Swanage Railway. It is seen passing sister No. 34070 *Manston* at Corfe Castle. Had the volunteers not reversed the post-Beeching closure of the Swanage branch, this location may well have been covered by a bypass. ANDREW PM WRIGHT

congestion. Worse still, parking spaces in Swanage and the picture-postcard tourist honeypot of Corfe Castle en route at the height of the season are often at a premium.

Here the revived railway now plays an enormous part in solving the problem, even though the part that carries regular public services is just 5¼ miles long.

A giant car park lies next to the western terminus of Norden, a stop that never existed in British Railways days or before. It lies around half a mile to the west of Corfe Castle.

Visitors leave their vehicles at the car park, built with funding from local authorities, and catch the train either the short distance to Corfe Castle or go all the way to Swanage, where the station is a very short walk from the beach.

No queues on sweltering summer days, no endless driving round and round to find a place to park – just sit back and relax and let the train take the strain.

Swanage is not the only resort in the country to benefit from rail park and ride – the St Ives branch in Cornwall immediately comes to mind, where a lack of parking spaces in the resort in the high season is notorious – but this one dangles the extra carrot of a ride behind a steam train. Heritage diesels and diesel multiple units play their part too, acting as people carriers at carnival and festival times when the overriding intention is to reach a destination rather than marvel at what is hauling the train. The railway has boasted that it runs the most intensive service of a UK heritage railway.

Locomotives which in Beeching's day were being consigned to the scrapyard are now serving a regular genuine public transport function once again.

Again, to maximise both its revenue and its usefulness to the Isle of Purbeck, the Swanage Railway has added modern-day intermediate stations.

Harman's Cross, a midway point, serves several caravan and camp sites, where holidaymakers see the trains as the most convenient way of getting around.

Norden station offers much more than a standard park-and-ride facility. It has become a transport hub served by buses which link it to other prime local tourist destinations, so someone who wanted to avoid using their car during a week's holiday could instead rely on public transport.

Now the railway is pressing ahead with moves to reinstate 'real' as opposed to 'heritage' services over the full length of the original branch to Wareham.

In volunteer-led revivalist terms, the Swanage Railway has blazed a trail for others to follow, and those who believe that British Railways closed it before its time felt vindicated every time passenger numbers rose yet again.

Yet the rebirth of the branch, which opened on May 20, 1885, has been far from plain sailing.

Starting again from scratch

The Swanage branch was not listed in the Beeching report of 1963, and so the blame for its closure cannot be laid directly at his door, although his pruning of the national network undoubtedly paved the way to that end.

British Rail wanted rid of the branch in 1966, but it was Barbara Castle, transport minister under Harold Wilson's Labour government (the same party which had pledged in 1964 to stop all the rail closures and reverse all of the Beeching cuts if it was voted into office) who sounded its death knell.

She decided, under the May 1967 Network for Development blueprint, that lines which made losses but served a social need could be retained, like the Bere Alston-Gunnislake section of the Callington branch on the border between Devon and Cornwall, saved because local topography makes car journeys a winding, tortuous affair by comparison. However, other loss-

making branches, including the Swanage branch, could be closed.

In late 1967 British Railways issued a notice to close the branch by the following September.

The notice caused local outrage and a public inquiry was held into the fact that there had been difficulty in arranging replacement bus services.

The Department of the Environment inspector heading the inquiry was presented with evidence that a replacement bus service would be unable to handle the traffic in the summer months.

He recommended that the line should stay open, but was overruled by the environment secretary.

The line was closed on January 1, 1972, and British Rail ordered the eastern two-thirds of the branch to be lifted soon afterwards. The westernmost part of the branch was retained as far as Furzebrook to serve the Wytch Farm petrol/gas terminal, which closed only in the 21st century.

Four months after the last train ran, the Swanage Railway Society was established, with the aim of rebuilding it.

It would be a mountain to climb. If you look at many of Britain's other top-flight major heritage railways, most of them started with a line where the track was still intact – the Severn Valley, Keighley & Worth Valley, West Somerset, South Devon, Dartmouth Steam for example. By comparison, the Swanage Railway had to begin from scratch with an empty trackbed.

In July 1975 a licence was granted by Swanage Town Council to the Swanage Railway Society to occupy the disused Swanage station site after the scheme received 83% support from local people in a referendum.

On February 13, 1976, a 12 month lease was signed for Swanage station. On May 8 that year, the first item of rolling stock arrived at Corfe Castle station in the form of LSWR coach body No. 0695. On June 26, the first locomotive arrived at Swanage station in the form of

ABOVE: A prime contender for the most majestic vista on any revived railway: the ruins of medieval Corfe Castle tower above the Swanage Railway, which has been restored to its former Southern Region glory. ANDREW P M WRIGHT

BELOW: Class 205 'Thumper' Diesel Electric Multiple Unit No. 1110 at Swanage station on the last day of public services under British Rail on January 1, 1972. BARRY THIRLWALL

WITHDRAWAL OF RAILWAY PASSENGER SERVICE BETWEEN WAREHAM AND SWANAGE

The Southern Region of British Railways hereby give notice that on and from Monday 3 January 1972 the railway passenger service between Wareham and Swanage will be withdrawn and Corfe Castle and Swanage stations closed.

Details of the alternative bus services are available at local railway stations and bus offices.

British Rail | Southern

ABOVE: : Swanage branch 1972 closure poster.
TONY TROOD

Planet petrol-mechanical four-wheeler *Beryl* from Corral's at Poole Quay. August 23 saw the first complete piece of rolling stock arrive at Swanage station in Southern Railway van No. 1234.

The first steam locomotive arrived on September 23 in the form of unrestored 1954-built BR Standard 4MT 2-6-4T No. 80078 from Dai Woodham's famous scrapyard at Barry.

In 1977, work started on the restoration of the Swanage station canopy, while on November 28 that year, Swanage Town Council issued a statement of intent letting the railway use the station site and buildings.

The following year, tracklaying from the northern end of Swanage goods shed began, and in March the first passenger carriage arrived at Swanage station in the form of 1940s Southern Railway Bulleid coach No. 4365.

The Southern Steam Trust, which manages the railway restoration project, was formed as a charity out of the old Southern Steam Group in 1978, and on February 1, 1979, the Swanage Railway Company was formed to operate the trains.

On March 3, 1979, the first fully working steam locomotive, a small Barclay oil burning 0-4-0ST named Richard Trevithick, arrived at Swanage. On August 6, the first passenger-carrying train since New Year's Day left Swanage and ran 200 yards to Northbrook road bridge. By the end of the summer season, around 30,000 people were carried.

In 1981, Dorset County Council leased the two miles of trackbed between Herston and Harman's Cross to the railway.

On Good Friday 1984, services had been extended to Herston Halt on the edge of the resort, a distance of a mile.

There followed a heated campaign to stop a Corfe Castle bypass being built on the vacant trackbed. Finally, on July 24, 1986, the county council voted not to build the bypass, which would have scuppered the revival of the branch.

Also in 1986, a group of supporters bought LSWR M7 0-4-4T No. 30053, a veteran of the Swanage branch, from a museum in Vermont, US. After its withdrawal in mid-May 1964, it had been sold abroad for preservation. Arriving back in April 1987, via Felixstowe Docks, it underwent a five-year restoration and returned to steam on the Swanage Railway in 1992.

In 1987, the revivalists secured a lease on trackbed as far as Furzebrook, and a Light Railway Order was obtained, empowering the railway to rebuild the line as far as Norden.

On September 11 that year, the 100,000th fare-paying passenger was carried on the Swanage Railway since the service to Herston Halt began in 1984. The passenger was carried from Swanage to the one and a half mile mark near New Barn.

In March 1989, Harman's Cross station was opened.

Operation Millstone

What had seemed to the outside world to be a classic case of plain sailing, a case of relaying track as fast as volunteers could physically manage, was anything but. By 1991, the railway found itself embroiled in a financial crisis after

ABOVE: Passengers on the last British Rail Swanage train at Wareham on New Year's Day 1972. It would take more than four decades to reverse the closure of the complete branch to passengers.
ARTHUR GRANT

BELOW: One of the last tickets issued by British Rail to travel on the Swanage branch on January 1, 1972.
PETER DOWNER

2nd - RETURN
FAREWELL RUN
SOUVENIR TICKET
1st JANUARY, 1972
Wareham to
SWANAGE
& BACK
(S) For conditions see over
0256   0256

plans to extend the railway from Harman's Cross to Corfe Castle spectacularly ran out of cash.

A £250,000 bank loan underwritten by the county council to pay for the extension had run out without the new track being ballasted and with much of the infrastructure incomplete.

Worse was to come. An auditor's letter leaked to volunteers said that not only were the accounts two years behind but they were also in a mess. It was discovered that operating body the Swanage Railway Company Ltd had accrued debts of more than £250,000, a figure which shocked even the sternest critics of the line's then-management.

The local planning authority had insisted that the railway was to be built to a terminus at Norden instead of Corfe Castle to avoid road congestion. Therefore, the completed extension from Harman's Cross to Corfe Castle could not be brought into use to raise desperately needed revenue.

The crisis deepened when it was discovered that the Light Railway Order necessary to run to Corfe Castle had not even been applied for by the line's operating company.

Insolvency practitioners were consulted. Their advice was short, sharp and to the point: wind up the railway and walk away.

Bills piled up high in the Swanage station offices. General manager Mel Norris resigned, all but one out of 13 paid staff were made redundant, and as no other heritage line was prepared to loan a locomotive to the debt-stricken railway, it was left with only the 1708 Trust's Midland Railway 'half cab' 1F 0-6-0T No 1708 to haul trains during the 1991 summer season.

When it seemed that it could be a matter of days before the railway went under, local businessman Bill Trite, who had worked voluntarily on the restoration of Bulleid Merchant Navy 4-6-2 No. 35027 *Port Line*, found himself at the head of an emergency committee formed to operate the line.

Members of the railway donated £50,000 to pay off creditors.

Bill pursued a new strategy of openness. He told every creditor just how bad the situation was, warts and all, while asking for more time to pay.

The peak summer season came, and was marked by several weeks of sunny starts to the day followed by lunchtime drizzle, driving sunbathers off the sands – and on to the trains. The pattern is echoed throughout the heritage railway movement: general managers across the country know only too well that rain sells tickets, because a preserved railway is a perfect all-weather attraction.

Restored BR Standard 4MT 2-6-4T No. 80078 was sold to a group of members and leased back to the railway, allowing a £32,000 bill to the taxman to be settled.

TOP: Disused Swanage station in 1975: no more than a bus stop. GEORGE MOON

ABOVE: Tracklaying begins at Swanage station in 1977. MICK STONE

BELOW: Swanage Railway pioneers pictured in 1977 at Swanage with their first items of motive power. MICK STONE

In short, a miracle was worked under the guidance of Bill Trite.

The new administration confounded the accountants and by that autumn many of the creditors had been paid.

The Swanage Railway Trust came up with a scheme whereby free travel for life could be obtained for £250, or £5 a month, and more than 1600 of these deals were taken up, reducing the £250,000 extension loan.

After a public inquiry, the Light Railway Order was granted in 1993, with Norden station opening on August 12, 1995. That year, the railway carried around 98,000 passengers.

The park-and-ride scheme was a winner from the start and the car park had to be extended several times to cater for demand. It earned the line the Heritage Railway Association's Annual Award for Excellence in 1998.

Under Bill Trite, in December 1995, the railway launched Operation Millstone in a bid to clear the overdraft. An appeal for donations was made to all members and a leaflet asking for contributions was placed on every seat on services trains in a handwritten envelope. Within a few years, all of the debts were paid off, and the railway has flourished under sound financial management ever since.

Reconnection to the main line

The next giant step forward for the Swanage Railway came on January 3, 2002, when the remaining missing sections of track separating the heritage line from the national network were laid between Norden and the Network Rail stopblock at Motala, a house to the east of Furzebrook sidings. It was 30 years from the exact date of closure of the line to Swanage that the revivalists reached

ABOVE: During its historic visit to the Swanage Railway in early May 2009, Bulleid 4-6-2 No. 34067 *Tangmere* double headed service trains with resident sister No. 34070 *Manston.* The back-to-back pair are seen departing Corfe Castle for Swanage. ROBIN JONES

the buffer stop at the far end of the headshunt of the Furzebrook liquid propane gas terminal freight-only stub of the original branch that had remained in situ.

Original members of the revival scheme and co-founder Andrew Goltz, who flew in from Poland, were present at the relinking event which took place next to Arland House, a bungalow between Stoborough and Corfe Castle.

After the heritage line's permanent way track gang led by Tony Andrews and Barry Light laid the final sections of track up to the stopblock, a special ceremonial gold-plated track screw was fixed into the final Swanage Railway sleeper by Andrew and Tony Trood of Wareham who maintained the Swanage branch line track when he worked for British Rail.

In a lineside speech, Bill Trite, who had by then been the railway's chairman for several years, said: "It took British Rail seven weeks to rip the track up from Swanage and 30 years for us to reconnect it." However, the half-

TOP RIGHT: A typical Beeching era scene replicated right across Britain: Corfe Castle station in 1985, devoid of tracks but the platforms and buildings still intact. ANDREW PM WRIGHT

ABOVE: Tracklaying at Corfe Castle in 1990. ANDREW PM WRIGHT

mile headshunt, the wooden sleepers and track which dated back to the steam era had been disused for many years, as evidenced by the liberal covering of thick gorse bushes. Wholesale clearance of vegetation over this section then had to take place if the reconnection was to become meaningful.

The railway was privately approached by Virgin Trains about the possibility of bringing a brand-new Voyager Class 221 Super Voyager unit to Swanage to be named – and photographed in that immortal setting running eastwards from Corfe Castle, arguably the most dramatic landscape in the UK heritage railway portfolio.

However, HM Railway Inspectorate stipulated that the train must be run as empty coaching stock and operate at no more than 5mph between Furzebrook and Motala.

Within days there were Swanage Railway volunteers queuing up to spend their summer holidays preparing the necessary trackwork to make it happen. Virgin sponsored part of the cost of restoring the overgrown

ABOVE: Corfe Castle station today: repatriated LSWR M7 0-4-4T No. 30053 in its newly applied lined BR livery heads a train to Swanage. ANDREW P M WRIGHT

RIGHT: More than 30 years after the last passenger train came this way from Wareham, Class 221 No. 220018 Dorset Voyager bursts through the celebratory banner at Norden on September 8, 2002. ANDREW P M WRIGHT

RIGHT: Rapturous crowds greet the arrival of Virgin Super Voyager No. 220018 Dorset Voyager at Swanage on September 8. ANDREW P M WRIGHT

RIGHT: Class 221 No. 220018 Dorset Voyager passes the 'Pines Express' hauled by Bulleid Battle of Britain Pacific No. 34072 257 Squadron at Harman's Cross. ANDREW P M WRIGHT

half-mile of track, which two staff from contractors Balfour Beatty had found could be returned to use if 150 sleepers were replaced.

On Sunday, September 8, 2002, the first through train from the main line at Wareham visited Swanage via a section of track which temporarily replaced the stopblock at Motala.

The bright summer sunshine and blue skies contrasted with a dull and overcast January 1, 1972, when Hampshire Class 3H DEMU No. 1110 made the last trips from Swanage to Wareham.

Back then, a mere handful of people boarded the workaday train liveried in BR corporate blue with double-arrow logo and yellow ends.

Three decades later, thousands of people lined the route to watch the glamorous shiny new Super Voyager slowly wind its way over the restored connection and on to the Swanage Railway.

By coincidence, the Voyager's trip on and off the recompleted branch was signalled by the man who signalled the final BR train from Swanage to Wareham on New Year's Day 1972.

Bob Richards was the last signalman at Corfe Castle station where he had started his railway career in 1962. On Monday, January 3, 1972, the day that the Swanage branch was officially closed, Bob started work at Wareham box.

Thirty years later, Bob was on duty at Wareham when the Virgin Voyager came through Wareham bound for Swanage on the Saturday evening, and on the Sunday evening when the Voyager ran back on to the national network.

The incoming Voyager's historic trip to Swanage also took place on the 40th anniversary of the last 'Pines Express' inter-regional cross country train running on the Somerset & Dorset Joint Railway main line between Bournemouth and Bath, one of the biggest victims of the Beeching Axe. On the day, Bulleid Battle of Britain

The perfect seaside destination: Swanage station today, with BR Standard 4MT 2-6-4T No. 80104 at the buffer stops. ANDREW P M WRIGHT

Today's scene is a dramatic contrast indeed with 1977. JOHN KELLAWAY

Pacific No. 34072 *257 Squadron* ran on the Swanage Railway with a 'Pines Express' headboard on the front, and with Peter Smith, who drove the last Up 'Pines' on the S&D, with his hand on the regulator.

Heading the 2.35pm train from Swanage, No. 34072 passed the Voyager – the first new inter-regional cross country train since the 'Pines Express' – at Harman's Cross station as the Class 221 was working the 2.35pm Norden to Swanage train.

Bill Trite, who officiated at the naming of the Class 221 as Dorset Voyager, summed up the driving force behind the revival of the Swanage Railway and that of other closed lines, both by preservationists and in other cases by local councils: "A small group of people who were determined to make this happen and they have been augmented by others over the years but always there has been a vision that has motivated the project.

"It is a vision that is quite independent of a rational appraisal of what is possible. In other words, it is determination winning over the principles of accountancy."

London on line again

After the English Civil War, Cromwell's roundheads ruined the domineering fortress of Corfe Castle so it could never be used in battle again. Now the revivalists had overturned the effects of another Castle – the Labour transport minister Barbara, during whose reign in power the closure plans had been formulated.

Work to improve the track continued over the next five years and a permanent groundframe and catchpoint

ABOVE: History was made on May 2, 2009, when Bulleid Battle of Britain Pacific No. 34067 *Tangmere* headed the 'Wessex Venturer' railtour over the main line link to the Swanage Railway at Motala and towards Cat's Eye bridge on the A351. ROBIN JONES

system was installed at Motala, so the reconnection could be permanent.

On May 10, 2007, a convoy of four diesel locomotives arriving for a gala became the first train movement to use this permanent connection from the main line.

Improvements to the track between Norden and Wareham allowed the planning and operation of special incoming railtour services for the first time since 1972.

The first public passenger service between Wareham and Swanage since 1972 was the 'Purbeck Pioneer', a 12-coach diesel-hauled railtour from London Victoria to Swanage via Wareham on April 1, 2009. Due to huge demand, the tour was repeated the next day.

Saturday, May 2, that year marked another watershed, when the reborn railway accepted its first incoming steam-hauled special. Rebuilt Bulleid Battle of Britain 4-6-2 No. 34067 *Tangmere* hauled the first through steam train to the Purbeck resort from London since 1967, at the head of Past-Time Rail's 'Wessex Venturer' from London Victoria. Train operator West Coast Railways supplied a maroon Class 37, No 37706, as motive power for the return journey at 4.10pm the same day.

The 10 coach train hauled by *Tangmere* left London Victoria on time at 8.05am, travelling to Swanage via Woking, Winchfield, for a watering stop, Basingstoke, Winchester, Eastleigh, Southampton, Brockenhurst, Bournemouth, Branksome, Poole and Hamworthy before arriving 15 minutes early at Wareham.

Spectators lined the route at crossings and stations, including Bournemouth, Poole and Wareham, and beyond there crowded every overbridge and other vantage point along the heritage line.

Approaching Corfe Castle, the special passed unrebuilt sister No. 34070 *Manston*, waiting in the loop with the next regular service to Norden.

Finally, the 'Venturer' pulled into Swanage, where, with the platform off limits because of the waiting VIP party and TV cameramen, there was standing room only

The new crossover at Wareham being completed in October 2012. It will allow Swanage Railway trains to access the town station. ANDREW P M WRIGHT

alongside the top of the embankment and on the pavement behind the buffer stops. Rebuilt West Country light Pacific No. 34028 *Eddystone* welcomed the visitor with two blasts of the horn while a crowd of more than 1000 cheered and applauded as *Tangmere* came to a stop at 1.17pm – just two minutes late after a journey of more than five hours.

On Monday, May 4, *Tangmere* headed Past-Time Rail's 'The Royal Wessex' trip, the first steam-hauled passenger train from Purbeck to Waterloo since Sunday, June 18, 1967.

It was the return leg of a journey which began at Waterloo behind diesel traction earlier that day.

Understandably, Swanage traders are only too happy to see around 500 extra visitors in the resort every time a charter train calls. That is over and above the tens of thousands of annual visitors who are lured into the resort by the presence of the heritage railway itself.

The final pieces in the jigsaw

Having special trains run over the national network to Swanage is, however, only the start of running regular services on and off the heritage line.

The biggest physical stumbling block that remained was the resignalling of Worgret Junction, the start of the branch, to allow regular as opposed to occasional stock movements. Another obstacle was the lack of automatic barriers costing £500,000 on petroleum giant BP's road to the Wytch Farm oil field at Norden, over which special trains had to be worked by flagmen stopping road traffic.

Furthermore, the big question arose about the future status of the line's heritage services if regular diesel services are introduced.

Outside train operating companies would want to run trains at a higher line speed than the currently permitted 25mph, to which the Swanage Railway, like most other heritage lines, is restricted under its Light Railway Order.

The railway's board has firmly pledged that steam and heritage diesel-hauled services will

not be jeopardised by the requirements of access to the line by outside operators.

One solution that has been considered was the building of an interchange station at Worgret Junction itself.

The Strategic Rail Authority conditionally endorsed a £6.8 million bid to reconnect the branch to the national network and restore through public services, but stipulated that the money must be paid through a train operating company such as South West Trains.

In 2010, Dorset County and Purbeck District councils together pledged £3 million for vital mainline resignalling work for a permanent year-round train service to run from Wareham to Swanage, as part of its Purbeck Transportation Strategy. Network Rail had scheduled the resignalling of the main London to Weymouth line between Poole and Wool during 2012 and if Worgret Junction was resignalled at the same time, it would cost only £3 million.

If the junction was instead resignalled at a later date, it could cost up to £10 million, well out of the heritage line's scope.

BP subsequently came on board big time with a £500,000 gift to finance the construction and maintenance of the automatic level crossing

The pivotal donation came after BP sold its majority shareholding in the Wytch Farm oilfield north of Corfe Castle – the largest onshore oilfield in Western Europe – to Anglo-French oil company Perenco during December.

Between October and December 2012, Worgret Junction was resignalled by Network Rail and trackwork laid including a new crossover at Wareham and a point at Worgret to facilitate the working of branch trains.

The total cost to both councils was £3.2 million and was funded by a transport infrastructure improvement tax levied on property developers in the Purbeck area – a facility not available in the Beeching era.

On February 11, 2013, a £1.47 million grant to the Swanage Railway for the purposes of reintroducing a regular train service to Wareham under the Government's Coastal Communities Fund was announced by Eric

Pickles, Secretary of State at the Department of Communities and Local Government.

The grant will pay for the upgrading of track and bridges on Network Rail's section of the branch from Worgret Junction to Furzebrook. It is intended that the first trains will run in the spring of 2015. The money will also finance the refurbishment of two DMU sets for the services and the acquisition of the necessary legal permissions.

A trial rail service between Swanage, Corfe Castle and Wareham is planned for 50 days in 2015 and 90 days in 2016 with the eventual target being an all-year amenity train service – if it shows that it can pay its way.

Present Swanage Railway Company chairman Peter Sills, who rode on the last train from Swanage to Wareham on January 1, 1972, as a teenager, said: "The grant from the Coastal Communities Fund will give an important transport, tourism and employment boost to the Isle of Purbeck as well as taking more cars off the road between Swanage, Corfe Castle, Wareham, Poole and Bournemouth.

"By providing a regular train service from Swanage and Corfe Castle to Wareham connecting with the South West Trains service between London and Weymouth, it will become much easier for people to use public transport which will improve employment opportunities for Purbeck residents and also increase the number of tourists visiting the Isle of Purbeck.

"Rail travel in this country has grown by a third during the past decade and train journeys are currently at their highest level since the 1920s. With petrol prices so high – and still rising – we are confident that a regular train service between Swanage and Wareham will be viable."

Fifty years on...

On March 26, 2013, just one day before the 50th anniversary of the 1963 Beeching report, which scuppered Dorset's Lyme Regis and Bridport branches, South West Trains ran its first passenger train from Bournemouth to Corfe Castle and Swanage, a one-off special

comprising Class 159 DMU No. 159015 to show dignitaries and stakeholders the progress being made towards reintroducing a regular amenity train service from Swanage to Wareham.

Steve Mackenzie, chief executive of Purbeck District Council, said: "It was a fantastic step forward for a modern passenger train to travel the full length of the Wareham to Swanage branch line.

The Swanage Railway conductor guiding the South West Trains driver between Motala and Swanage was founder Swanage Railway member and volunteer Bob McGaw of Wareham – one of the team that gained access to the boarded up Swanage station on that cold bleak day back in February 1976.

Negotiations are under way for the Swanage Railway to take over Network Rail's section of the branch, making it complete in every respect once more.

What does the future hold?

Despite the hiccup of 1991, the Swanage Railway has become a fairytale success story of what can be achieved if enough local people are determined to restore and reopen their branch line.

While there are many closed branches that have been revived as heritage railways, line museums and major tourist attractions in their own right, few if any can be said to have progressed this far in terms of restoring real public services.

However, can they be made to pay?

Running seasonal trains to the seaside is the railway's forte. With many of the other seaside branch lines closed by Beeching and his successors, the ability of such lines to pay during the peak season was rarely in doubt. It was the lack of patronage throughout the rest of the year, coupled with the cost of storing coaches out of season, which plunged the balance books into the red and led to the closures.

In these far more enlightened times as far as public transport is concerned, can the Swanage Railway do any better in 2013 than the Southern Region did in the mid-Sixties?

It is difficult to see how, for instance, an all-the-year-round six-times-a-day DMU service from Swanage to Wareham and back could pay. A properly promoted rush-hour service, and one on market days, could well be a different matter entirely.

Travelling by rail is a long-winded way of getting from Swanage to Poole and Bournemouth. The shortest distance by far is to drive or take the bus from Swanage to Studland and catch the vehicle ferry over the mouth of Poole Harbour to Sandbanks. That is all very well, but lengthy time-consuming queues build up on either side of the ferry at peak periods. A train trip may be seen as an attractive and time-saving alternative.

Regular through running to Wareham would certainly make Swanage commutable to places beyond Bournemouth and Poole.

It will almost certainly increase its attractiveness as a residential and retirement location.

Who knows – the return of the railway might even see the resort emulate the millionaires' row of Sandbanks and see property prices soar.

Either way, with the Swanage Railway in the driving seat, the heritage services, the core plank of its business, will be protected.

Many eyes will be on the railway in the years to come. It is likely to be viewed as a test bed for other coastal or multi-use railway revival schemes, and as such could play an integral part in the rebirth of branch lines elsewhere.

It may decide whether or not a business case can be formed for other seaside branches, which fell into decline with the advent of cheap package overseas holidays in the Eighties and Nineties, and have now reinvented themselves as round-the-year destinations for short breaks, or highly-desirable places to live and commuter from in their own right.

ABOVE: The 'Purbeck Adventurer', a special day excursion from Windsor to Corfe Castle on June 29, comprised South West Trains Class 159 DMUs Nos. 159006/9. It was the first train from London to use the bay platform since Swanage station opened in 1885. It was also the first passenger train via Wareham to use the bay platform since September 4, 1966, when regular British Rail steam trains on the branch ended. The bay platform was specially refurbished for the six-car charter. ANDREW P M WRIGHT

Deltic D9007 *Pinza* heading a Railway Correspondence & Travel Society farewell tour at Riccarton Junction on January 5, 1969. COLOUR-RAIL

Waverley Route:
The biggest Beeching reversal of all

Dr Beeching said the Waverley Route between Carlisle and Edinburgh was "the biggest money loser in the British railway system".

Fifty years after his report was published, the axing of the 98 mile trunk route from Edinburgh to Carlisle was the worst of all the Beeching cuts according to author and railway expert David Spaven.

The closure left the Scottish Borders as the only region of Britain without rail.

Hawick (population 14,801), 56 miles from Edinburgh and 42 miles from Carlisle, is the largest town farthest from a railway station. Nowadays, buses link the town to the railway station at Carlisle.

Beeching had a clear choice. There are two main routes from the West Coast Main Line to Edinburgh – one from Carlisle,

running through sparsely or uninhabited hill country for much of the way, with several significant gradients, or a shorter route from Carstairs Junction, which is further north and goes through a far more densely-populated area. With elimination of duplicate routes, one of his major goals in his bid to create an inter-city network that would pay its way, there was no surprise as to which one he chose.

In 1963, the Edinburgh Waverley-Hawick-Carlisle route was listed for complete withdrawal of passenger services. Its eventual closure sparked one of the biggest debates of the post-Beeching era, and left much anger in the towns that were disenfranchised from the rail network.

Now, however, the trains are coming back, if only over part of the line.

The line was built by the North British Railway, opening from Edinburgh to Hawick in 1849 and extending to Carlisle in 1862.

A double-track main line throughout, it was named the Waverley Route after the Waverley novels by Sir Walter Scott.

The route's marked features were its steep gradients and bleak moorland terrain, and it was often said to be the most difficult line in the UK for steam locomotives to work over.

Long before Beeching, passengers and freight were switching to road transport, and many of the line's branches saw passenger services withdrawn – Galashiels to Selkirk on September 8, 1951; Riccarton to Hexham on October 15, 1956; and Kelso to Tweedmouth on June 13, 1964.

By 1954, 80% of livestock from local farms was being carried by lorry, and by 1963 the last

cattle traffic had disappeared from the line. Road transport also took over the local woollen and tweed business.

Express trains in the 1950s took around two-and-a-half hours to cover the distance from Carlisle to Edinburgh. The locomotives designated to the route were usually LNER A3 Pacifics, which were unsuited to the gradients as they had been designed for long lengths of 80mph running on the East Coast Main Line with heavy express trains.

By contrast, the 'Waverley' express was typically eight coaches and the Waverley Route was 70mph maximum with many tight curves limited to much lower speed. Climbing from Newcastleton to Whitrope Summit, an A3-hauled express would be down to 30mph by Steele Road, with the locomotive being worked flat out.

Beeching worked out that the last two daily St Pancras to Edinburgh expresses and the freight trains could go via other routes. Take them away and only the local passenger trains services were left. On the bleak, southern part of the route – where next to nobody lived – the figures would never stack up.

The statutory closure notices were posted at all stations on the line in October 1966, stating that services would be withdrawn from January 2, 1967.

ABOVE: St Margarets-shedded LNER V2 2-6-2 No. 60892 near Melrose on an Edinburgh to Carlisle stopper in the late 1950s. AC CAWSTON/ JOHN S WHITELEY COLLECTION

Because 508 official objections were lodged against the closure within the required six weeks of the closure notice being issued, a reprieve was announced and the closure was postponed pending review, which resulted in a public hearing being held in Hawick on November 16-17, 1967.

However, on July 15, 1968, Richard Marsh, Labour Minister for Transport, announced that the line would close on January 6, 1969.

The protests intensified, and even William Ross, the Secretary of State for Scotland, added his voice. Local MP David Steel, who was elected leader of the Liberal party in 1976, also became a focal point of the protests. He was just 26 when he was elected to Parliament in a by-election in 1965, called after the previous pro-Beeching report Conservative MP had died.

Steel lobbied ministers and British Railway officials to keep the line open as a branch line serving Borders towns.

Local people collected a petition and a delegation went to London on December 18, 1968, to present it to 10 Downing Street, but Marsh refused to budge. British Rail claimed that the route's losses were too great.

In a letter to David Steel, Marsh said that the Waverley Route was the most unprofitable main line in the country. Returns showed that it cost 1s-4d (7p) for each passenger mile on this route compared to an average of 3d (1½p)

per passenger mile throughout Britain. Also, the number of passengers using the line had slumped during the previous few years.

Estimates of the annual losses that would be incurred by running a basic service ranged from £215,000-£700,000.

The Government admitted that in the Border areas there was a strong case for retention on the grounds of hardship.

Lord Shepherd, the Minister of State for Overseas Affairs, told the House of Lords that the 'Borderers' had every sympathy over the loss of the line. However, it failed to qualify for a share of the £10 million which the Labour Government had allocated to support unprofitable lines in Scotland where social grounds were a factor.

An independent report by London transport economist John Hibbs, commissioned by 14 local authorities in the area, suggested that they should form

a consortium, along with Edinburgh, to operate the line from Hawick themselves, but the idea was not well received. It also said that a subsidy would be required.

Banner and placard-waving campaigners turned out in force during the weekend that the line was closed. British Rail ran a 'Farewell to the Waverley Route' special, while another was charted by the Border Union Railway Society, which had formed to try to save the line.

The society special, hauled by Class 55 Deltic D9002 *The King's Own Yorkshire Light Infantry*, now preserved and owned by the National Railway Museum, carried a coffin bearing the inscription 'Waverley Line – born 1849, killed 1969'.

The last passenger service on the line – also the final train to run over the entire route – was 1M82, the 9.56pm Edinburgh-St Pancras sleeper train on Sunday, January 5, 1969, hauled by Class 45 diesel D60 Lytham St Annes.

The points were tampered with at Hawick to delay the train and a Clayton diesel, D8506, was despatched in front of the sleeper service to make sure that the route southwards was safe.

The pilot engine found that it was unable to proceed beyond Newcastleton because the level crossing gates had been padlocked. More than 200 protestors turned out and, led by local vicar the Rev Brydon Maben, stood on the tracks with placards reading 'Stop the Great Train Robbery', 'No Trains No Jobs' and 'Don't Cut Our Lifeline'.

The vicar was among those arrested and was released only after David Steel – later The Lord Steel of Aikwood, who had boarded the train at Galashiels – intervened and addressed the protestors. This delay caused 1M82 to arrive two hours late in Carlisle.

Lord Steel said: "The train got stopped at Newcastleton because the people in the village had closed the level crossing gates and were standing across the line.

ABOVE: Haymarket-based A3 Pacific No. 60096 *Papyrus* passes Bowland, just north of Galashiels, heading a St Pancras to Edinburgh overnight express in the mid/late-1950s. AC CAWSTON/JOHN S WHITELEY COLLECTION

BELOW: Passengers from the farewell special brave the wintry weather of January 5, 1969, to inspect Riccarton Junction for the last time. TREVOR GREGG

"I was summoned by the guard and had to get dressed and come out and address the people from the footbridge.

"It was freezing cold as it was well past midnight in early January, but they were minded not to go and police arrested the parish minister, the Rev Brydon Maben, who was one of the ringleaders of the demonstration, and that made things even more irresolute.

"The police tried to force the gates open, but they could not do anything and eventually I came to an agreement with the crowd that if I could get the minister released from the police station without charges they would go away.

"I think it is the only case of where the Edinburgh-London train was held up by the populous. It shows the level of anger and determination they had."

Rubbing salt in the wounds, on the afternoon of January 8 at Riddings Junction, British Rail staged a tracklifting 'ceremony' for the press, to split the London Midland and Scottish Regions, demonstrating their determination to dismantle the route.

The section from Newtongrange remained open for goods traffic as far as Hawick until April 28, 1969, the stretch from Lady Victoria colliery to Newtongrange lasting until December 20, 1971, and the final section – Newtongrange to Millerhill – closing on June 28, 1972. However, the parcels office at Hawick remained open so that British Rail vans could still carry parcels, but only by road.

German Pacifics to Edinburgh?

Immediately in the wake of the last train in 1969, a group was formed to try to take the Waverley Route over privately and run it using imported German Pacifics.

A holding company, under the name of the Border Union Railway Company, was founded to negotiate with British Rail for the purchase of the line.

One of the directors and the main protagonist was none other than TV presenter Bob Symes, also known as Robert Symes-Shutzmann, the stage name of inventor Robert Alexander Baron Schutzmann von Schutzmansdorff, who is descended from an Austrian aristocratic family.

The company, which gained support from David Steel and also the South of Scotland Chamber of Commerce, expressed confidence that it could break even in running the line.

It reiterated the protestors' argument that with a planned increase of 25,000 in the Border population, along with new industrial development, the railway would pick up new business if promoted. Symes said that tourist traffic could be attracted from the Lake District and from the Edinburgh end by running steam-hauled tours over the middle section of the route, while using diesels for commuter services.

As a BBC producer, he said that TV companies wanted suitable railway lines for location filming, and the Waverley fitted the bill.

The company was confident that trains could be run by the end of the year.

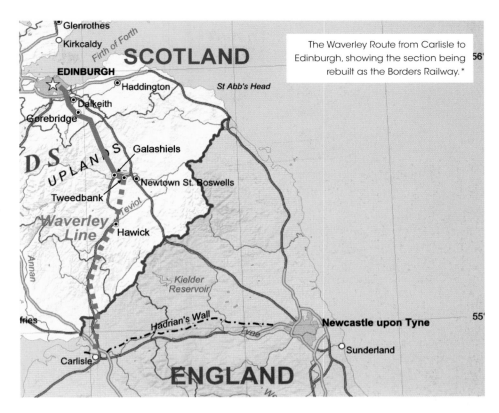

The Waverley Route from Carlisle to Edinburgh, showing the section being rebuilt as the Borders Railway. *

In November 1969, British Rail demanded a deposit of £250,000. When the company asked for extra time to find the money, the reply was that four months would be given, but interest of £8000 a month would have to be paid.

The talks concluded two days before Christmas. It seemed that British Rail had been placing every possible obstacle in the way of the revivalists, and many thought that the 'powers that were' simply did not want a private operator running a main line.

Several ideas were suggested to keep the route open, such as singling large sections and reducing the number of signalboxes. There was also the notion of a Waverley Route 'lite' offering just a basic DMU service to Edinburgh from Hawick.

Local authorities were also approached before and after closure to financially support a basic train service; but no support was forthcoming.

On January 6, 1970, British Rail formally announced that no agreement had been reached, after which the Border Union Railway Company quickly died a death.

An inspection saloon ran over the route on April 1, 1970, as part of preparation to allow contractors to bid for the demolition work.

Symes still managed to run a live steam railway on his own – in the back garden of his home in Guildford, built to 10¼in gauge.

In the 1970s, he presented his own Model World BBC programme dedicated to modelling, and in the 1990s co-presented a BBC TV series called Making Tracks dedicated to little-known lines and networks worldwide, and which specialised in steam operations.

In January 2007 he married Dr Sheila Gunn, then works manager at Boston Lodge on the Ffestiniog Railway. He is also the president of a Guildford-based model railway society called Astolat MRC.

ABOVE: Protestors demonstrate at the closure of the Waverley Route and the intransigence of the Labour Government over the issue. NRM

The slow way back

In the late 1990s, there was talk about reopening the southern section from Carlisle as far as Riccarton Junction, to extract timber from Kielder Forest.

With local roads seen as unable to cope with a significantly increased logging traffic, relaying a single track to carry the logs out by rail was seen as benefiting local communities, but the idea quickly faded away.

Borders people had, however, fought hard to keep their railway in vain, and even with the passing of a generation, they would still be quick to support any serious revival plan.

In January 1999, the Campaign for Borders Rail was formally launched at a Burns Supper in Melrose station, and collected thousands of signatures on a petition pressing for a rail route to the region to be relaid.

An independent study published in February 2000 stated that the reopening of the Borders rail link could be financially viable. The Scottish Executive's Transport Minister Sarah Boyack said that a funding proposal for a project estimated to cost £100 million should be developed.

On June 1, 2000, the Scottish Parliament debated whether to rebuild the entire Waverley Route.

In March 2003, the revivalist Waverley Railway Partnership produced research which claimed that a

ABOVE: Looking northwards from the north end of Carlisle Citadel station, where seven pre-Grouping railways came together. Here, the 6.22pm local from Langholm – headed by LMS Ivatt 4MT 2-6-0 No. 43139 – arrives as LNER Thompson A2/1 Pacific No. 60507 *Highland Chieftain* waits to leave on the 7.44am semi-fast to Edinburgh Waverley. BEN BROOKSBANK*

railway restored at a cost of up to £130 million would generate a minimum of £4.1 million in its first year, when around 5000 daily journeys would be made. Furthermore, reinstatement would lead to £130 million of housing investment in the Borders and Midlothian.

On January 6, 2005, marking the 36th anniversary of the last passenger train, a rally was held calling for the Waverley Route to be rebuilt. Six months later, a Scottish Parliament committee supported reinstatement of the northern 35 miles from Edinburgh to Galashiels.

In June the following year, members of the Scottish Parliament gave the green light to the Waverley Railway Bill to restore the Borders rail link between Edinburgh and Tweedbank near Galashiels. An overwhelming majority rejected the idea of rebuilding the line in stages to cut costs.

On March 27, 2007, work began to examine the formation of the old line prior to its rebuilding, the project then estimated to cost £155 million. A year later, it emerged that the line could cost twice as much to build as initially thought, and the schedule for completion had moved back from 2011 to 2013.

Labour MSPs criticised a decision to set up a non-profit making company to pay for the bulk of the costs, now estimated at up to £295 million.

LEFT: A young David Steel MP presented the petition against the Waverley Route closure to Prime Minister Harold Wilson at 10 Downing Street in December 1969. NRM

RIGHT: A coffin lamenting the death of the Waverley Route was despatched aboard this farewell special to Transport Minister Richard Marsh. NRM

Scottish Transport Minister Stewart Stevenson visited Galashiels on March 4, 2010, cutting the first sod of the new railway and thereby activating the Act of Parliament under which the railway is to be rebuilt.

Stevenson said that the new Borders Railway could spark economic growth across southern Scotland.

On June 21 that year, three organisations were chosen to tender for the project, the completion date now having moved back to 2014. However, the Scottish Government announced on September 29, 2011, that it had ditched its plan to get a private company to build the new railway because of a lack of interest.

Transport Minister Keith Brown said that the £295 million scheme would be taken forward with Network Rail, which subsequently stated that the opening date for the new line will be June 2015, after ScotRail drivers had undergone route learning.

Campaign for Borders Rail chairman Simon Walton said: "The scope of the project is huge, not made any easier by decisions made many decades ago to dismantle the infrastructure and not fully protect the right of way.

"The Borders Railway is a vastly better engineered project than the old Waverley Route. This is not simply a case of relaying railway lines."

David Spaven, author of Waverley Route: The Life, Death and Rebirth of the Borders Railway, said: "Transforming 30½ miles of abandoned line of route, 121 bridges and two tunnels into a fast, safe and sustainable transport link is a very substantial engineering task – in fact the longest rail reopening project in modern British history."

In December 2012, Network Rail appointed BAM Nuttall as the main contractor for the Borders Railway, with a £220 million contract. At 2012 prices, the total cost of the project has been given as £294 million.

David Simpson, Network Rail route managing director for Scotland, said: "The appointment of BAM Nuttall as our main contractor signals the start of the delivery of the new railway for the communities it will serve."

Transport Minister Keith Brown added: "The awarding of this contract so quickly after Network Rail took over delivery of the Borders Railway is a huge step forward for this vital project."

The project includes 30½ miles of new railway with new stations at Shawfair, Eskbank, Newtongrange, Gorebridge, Stow, Galashiels and Tweedbank. Around 90% of the line reuses the alignment of the Waverley Route.

On July 26, 2013, Scottish Borders Council leader David Parker helped mark the start of building work on Tweedbank station and its extensive park and ride facilities.

He said: "This is another great landmark for the Borders Railway project. Tweedbank station will be vital to the Scottish Borders economy and to local residents. As well as creating employment opportunities, it will allow access to existing workplaces in the area and it will form an important new transport hub for accessing the Borders General Hospital.

"With extra-long platforms, the station will have the capacity to bring excursion trains, many of which will bring tourists to nearby Melrose and beyond.

"I am already looking forward to the first trains arriving in 2015."

The Campaign for Borders Rail hopes that the entire route between Edinburgh and Carlisle will eventually be restored.

Chairman Simon Walton said: "The campaign remains committed to lobbying for the further restoration of the line to continue, past Tweedbank and on to Melrose and Hawick, with the full route to Carlisle as an ultimate aim."

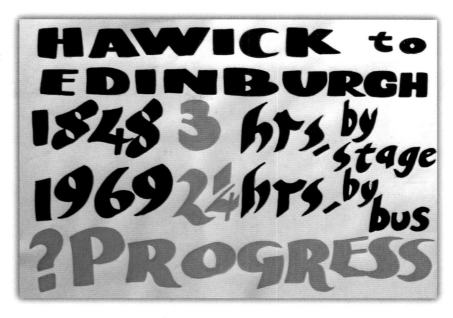

He said the group was pleased to read that the Scottish Government has recommended that the restoration of the complete route remains on the South East Scotland strategic planning agenda.

"Though some may consider the work of the Campaign for Borders Rail to be completed, we believe we have, so far, made a very good start," Mr Walton added.

In August 2013, it was reported that developers and property buyers alike were driving a housing boom along the Borders Railway corridor, with the number of new homes built in Midlothian more than doubling in the space of a year.

New houses completed in 2012 rose to 916 from 451 the year before. The surge in housebuilding nearly equalled the number of houses – 1097 – built across the whole of Edinburgh for the year.

Around 400 of the new houses were being built in areas located immediately along the revived route. Buyers include people who work in the Scottish capital but want to live in the countryside, a pattern repeated across Britain since the dawn of the railway network, and a lesson for other areas where lossmaking lines were closed by Beeching and his successors, but which now have populations capable of making them pay.

Ron Hastings, managing partner of real estate agency Hastings & Co, said enquiries about residential property

ABOVE: Returning steam trains to the line is the group's next goal.

BELOW: Placards waved at Westminster in protest at the closure. NRM

ABOVE: Experimental British Rail railbus RB004 prepares to depart the modern-day Whitrope Sidings station. TREVOR GREGG

close to the 35 miles of track had soared by 50% in the first six months of 2013, while average property prices rose by 3.2%.

A Network Rail spokesman said: "It is often the case that the opening of a new railway line can be a catalyst for the development of towns along the route, thus contributing to rising house prices."

The biggest unravelling of Beeching so far is now well under way.

The heritage approach

Trains are already running once again on part of the southern section of the Waverley Route, which is not part of the current Borders Railway scheme.

At Whitrope Siding, just short of the 1208 yard Whitrope Tunnel, south of Hawick, about half a mile of track has been relaid by the Waverley Route Heritage Association, which has also developed a heritage centre.

It was here at the top of the 1-in-75 climb from Hawick to the north, or the 1-in-80 climb from Newcastleton to the south, that banking engines would be removed and enter the siding before their next banking duties.

Whitrope never had a platform and was not classified as a station until, surprisingly, it was listed in the 1968 closure notice. It was officially a halt for railway staff only, but passengers could board trains by using a stepladder.

Formed in 2001, the association is aiming to extend its running line to Riccarton Junction two miles to the south. It was there that the North British Railway's Border Counties ran through Kielder, Bellingham and Reedsmouth to Hexham on the Tyne Valley. A railway village sprang up around the junction, which otherwise was sited in the middle of nowhere.

The North British built extensive facilities at Riccarton comprised a three-road engine shed capable of accommodating six locomotives, a carriage shed, coaling stage and a 55ft turntable.

On July 1, 2012 – the 150th anniversary of the opening of the line between Carlisle and Hawick – the association began running passenger trains over the short distance between Whitrope Station and Bridge 200 using British Rail Leyland National railbus demonstrator RB004, on loan from Northumbria Rail.

The official opening of the heritage centre in July 2010 was performed by Michael Moore, Liberal Democrat MP for Berwickshire, Roxburgh and Selkirk and the new Secretary of State for Scotland, and Madge Elliot, the veteran Borders rail campaigner who led the fight to save the Waverley Route in the late 1960s.

BELOW: The system map showing the new Borders Railway. SCOTRAIL

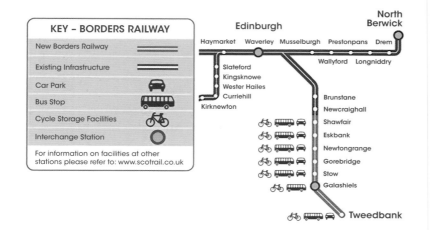

KEY – BORDERS RAILWAY	
New Borders Railway	═══
Existing Infrastructure	═══
Car Park	🚗
Bus Stop	🚌
Cycle Storage Facilities	🚲
Interchange Station	◯

For information on facilities at other stations please refer to: www.scotrail.co.uk

North Berwick

Edinburgh

Haymarket Waverley Musselburgh Prestonpans Drem

Slateford
Kingsknowe Wallyford Longniddry
Wester Hailes
Curriehill Brunstane
Kirknewton Newcraighall
Shawfair
Eskbank
Newtongrange
Gorebridge
Stow
Galashiels

Tweedbank

ABOVE: Transport Minister Keith Brown formally marking the start of the main works on the Borders Railway at the site of new Shawfair station. On his left is David Simpson, route managing director of Network Rail Scotland. NETWORK RAIL

LEFT: The trackbed cleared at the site of the new Tynehead station. RICHARD WEBB

ABOVE: The ruined stationmaster's house at Riccarton Junction. Much of the railway village which sprang up around this hitherto very isolated and bleak spot has gone the same way. ANDREW CUNNINGHAM*

ABOVE: Double track back on the Waverley Route southern section, at Whitrope Sidings. ANDREW CUNNINGHAM*

ABOVE: Ground stabilisation work at Monktonhall in January 2013 to address any problems caused by mining in the area. NETWORK RAIL

LEFT: The Waverley Route trackbed being cleared at Newtongrange in readiness for ballast laying. NETWORK RAIL

BELOW: Heavy plant moves into the site of Newtongrange station in April 2013. NETWORK RAIL

Chapter Fifteen

Revivalists' graduation
Rebuilding the Varsity Line

The Varsity Line between Oxford and Cambridge was not directly a victim of the Beeching Axe: indeed, it was a surprising omission from The Reshaping of British Railways.

British Railways wanted to close the 77 mile cross-country route as early as 1959, and Transport Minister Ernest Marples, the man who appointed Beeching, also wanted rid of it, and yet when the 1963 report presented the opportunity to close it, it was not taken. By inference it seems that Beeching saw merit in keeping an east-west route.

What did kill off the route was the provision of faster services between the two premier university cities via London, with the replacement of steam modern diesel trains.

The Oxford-Bicester-Bletchley-Bedford-Sandy-Cambridge line with its numerous stops was far more direct, but the focusing on inter-city services by British Rail in the wake of the Beeching rationalisation of the network meant that it was quicker to go the long way round.

The last passenger services over the route ran on New Year's Eve 1967, and it was officially closed the following day.

History

The Oxford to Cambridge route was an amalgamation of several sections built between 1850 and 1862.

The first of these was the Buckinghamshire Railway, which ran from Banbury via Buckingham to Bletchley and opened on March 30, 1850.

The following year the Buckinghamshire Railway opened a branch to Oxford from Verney Junction, named after the company's chairman, the Member of Parliament Sir Harry Verney, whose wife was Florence Nightingale's sister.

A temporary terminus at Banbury Road on the outskirts of Oxford was opened on December 2, 1850, while negotiations were under way to acquire land for the extension into the city.

The new terminus was built on the site of Rewley Abbey, a Cistercian monastery that dated from 1287.

It was designed in the same style as the Crystal Palace, built for the Great Exhibition in London in 1851, and used similar components too – prefabricated cast iron bolt-together sections.

To reach Oxford the line had to cross the Oxford Canal on its approach to the terminus and the railway company was forced to build a number of bridges including a swing bridge over the Sheepwash Channel, a navigable link between the Oxford Canal and the River Thames. The line into Oxford was opened on May 20, 1851.

Next came the Sandy & Potton Railway, a three mile line built by local landowner Captain William Peel, third son of former Prime Minister Sir Robert Peel, in the wake of the opening of Sandy station on the Great Northern Railway, in 1850.

The three mile line was opened for freight on June 25, 1857, and passengers in November that year. It was worked by an 0-4-0 saddle tank called *Shannon* built by George England & Company of Hatcham in London – which also supplied the world's first narrow gauge steam engines to the Ffestiniog Railway in 1863. It was named after the ship that Captain Peel commanded.

Shannon later ran on the Wantage Tramway and is preserved at Didcot Railway Centre.

The Sandy & Potton Railway was acquired by the Bedford & Cambridge Railway in 1860,

GWR Collett 61XX 2-6-2T No. 6126 at Islip with a Locomotive Club of Great Britain railtour on August 15, 1965. COLOUR RAIL

which intended to make the route part of a longer line to Cambridge. The track was relaid and Potton station was resited to the north.

The Bedford & Cambridge Railway opened throughout in 1862.

The London & North Western Railway worked the Buckinghamshire Railway on a 999 year lease from July 1, 1851, and absorbed the company on July 21, 1879.

The LNWR took over the Bedford & Cambridge Railway in 1865. However, it did not introduce a through service between Oxford and Cambridge, but ran separate Bletchley-Oxford and Bletchley-Cambridge services. That arrangement continued after 1923 under the LMS.

During the Second World War, the line was regularly used by trains running to and from the Bicester Military Railway. To facilitate them, a junction between the route and the Great Central Main Line was built between Calvert and Claydon.

In 1951, passenger trains were rerouted into Great Western Railway Oxford station, relegating the magnificent Rewley Road terminus to freight use.

British Railways' Railway Modernisation Plan of 1955 proposed improvements in cross-country facilities between Oxford and Cambridge with the aim of maintaining a link between the major main line railways outside the congested Greater London area, allowing freight traffic to be transferred between three railway regions and relieving the burden on London marshalling yards.

It was proposed to develop the Varsity Line as a freight link from the East Coast ports to South Wales, capable of handling up to 2400 wagons of coal class traffic and empties daily. These plans included the redevelopment of the sidings and land near Swanbourne station as a marshalling yard where trains could be sorted into the order required for their destinations on the Southern and Western Regions. The move would enable smaller goods yards in those regions to be closed, with the freight traffic concentrated at Swanbourne, which would be equipped with the latest automation technology.

In September 1958, work started on the upgrade of the Varsity Line with the construction of a flyover at Bletchley to separate local and long distance traffic. Compulsory purchase orders were issued for the proposed Swanbourne site including Horwood House, then a boarding school, which was earmarked by British Railways to become a training school for the new yard.

Gerry Fiennes was appointed as British Railways' chief operating officer in 1961 and opposed the scheme. He took the view that it was not justified either from the point of view of existing or potential traffic, and refused to send any East Coast Main Line traffic there.

At the time, the need for marshalling yards was in question as the movement of goods traffic by the wagonload was gradually being rationalised in favour of the liner train system which would not require the extensive storage facilities provided by marshalling yards. When the scheme was scuppered, Horwood House was given to the General Post Office.

All that survives of the plan is the Bletchley flyover.

The attempt made to close the Oxford-Cambridge line in 1959 failed due to overwhelming local opposition. The objectors were naturally delighted to find it omitted from the Beeching report of 1963.

At the time, it seemed the route figured in the reshaping plans for the national network, but others in the corridors of power disagreed. The campaigners were left utterly dismayed when, a year later, British Railways published closure plans for the whole route, still very much under the doctor's tenure. It has been said that road hauliers had been among those supporting the closure.

In 1966, the Great Central Main Line lost its passenger services north of Aylesbury, reducing traffic on the adjoining Varsity Line.

British Railways withdrew passenger services from the Oxford-Bletchley section of the Varsity Line on December 31, 1967, along with all trains from the Bedford-Cambridge section. That left just the middle section between Bletchley and Bedford in passenger use.

ABOVE: The Varsity's Line's original Oxford terminus, Rewley Road. A sister building to the Crystal Palace, it has been relocated to the Buckinghamshire Railway Centre at Quainton Road station. ROBIN JONES

BELOW: The LNWR's 77 mile 'Varsity Line', so named because it linked the university cities of Oxford and Cambridge. Only the sections in black were operational or in passenger use in 2013.

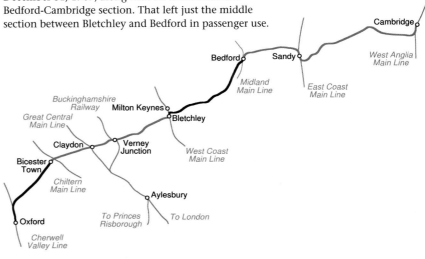

ABOVE: A First Great Western Class 165 unit emerges from Wolvercote Tunnel near Oxford.

The rundown had also set in here. All the stations lost their goods and parcels facilities and every one became an unstaffed halt from July 15, 1968.

British Rail came up with plans to close this last section from October 1972.

A mass of objections led to the closure being postponed until December 31 that year, to give sufficient time for a replacement bus service to be laid on.

The Bedford Rail Users' Association was formed to save the line and forced British Rail to postpone the closure pending an appeal.

By this time, there was a sea change in Government thinking over local rail services, and a change in legislation over subsidies to lines saved the route from closure. Whitehall offered a grant towards maintaining the service as part of the development of Milton Keynes, which itself did much to attract new passengers.

BELOW: By 2015, Chiltern railways will be able to run turbo trains like this Class 165 unit seen at Amersham on September 8, 2013, on new fast services from Oxford to Marylebone using an upgraded Varsity Line western section.
ROBIN JONES

ABOVE: By 2019, this overgrown cutting at Winslow, with track still in place in September 2013, will be carrying fast trains between Oxford and Bedford. ROBIN JONES

A 20 year contract between the Greater London Council and the London Brick Company worth £10 million to British Rail was signed in 1973 and assured the line's future. Under it, lock trains ran between new sidings at Stewartby and a new handling depot at Hendon.

On December 4, 2006, work began at Milton Keynes Central to prepare for a service connection from the Marston Vale Line.

Elsewhere, campaigners took a different but less successful approach to saving their local part of the Varsity Line.

The idea of preserving the line between Sandy and Potton was discussed at a public meeting at Sandy. It led to the formation of the Sandy & Potton Steam Railway Society.

It set out to buy the three mile line and run it as a heritage railway. However, the price asked by British Rail was too high, and despite the support of Sandy Urban District Council, the scheme fizzled out. Track lifting began in 1969, and left with the prospect of having to relay it by itself, the society was eventually wound up.

The Oxford-Bletchley section was mothballed but kept operational for rail freight travelling between the Western and Midland regions, empty stock movements and occasional excursion trains during the Seventies and Eighties enthusiasts' specials, which occasionally picked up at disused Winslow station. The intermediate stations were demolished or allowed to decay.

In the 1980s, the line between Aylesbury and Bletchley via Calvert was used for transfers of empty passenger rolling stock due to the closure of the Marylebone depot, when the maintenance of Network SouthEast Chiltern Lines' Class 115s was transferred to Bletchley. This ended with the opening of a new depot in Aylesbury and the introduction of the Class 165s. During 1982 the entire length of the Bletchley-Oxford section, which was then still double track throughout, was used for diverting Birmingham to Paddington via Coventry passenger services for three days while a bridge at Hill Wooton between Coventry and Leamington was replaced.

The last passenger train to operate on the Calvert to Bletchley section of the route was the 'Mothball Tour' in 1993, just before the line was taken out of use.

ABOVE: Class 37 No. 37038 with a test train heads west on Bletchley flyover for Newton Longville. PHIL MARSH

The way back

Calls to reopen the route never died away. The first target of pro-rail campaigners was the Oxford to Bicester Town section, which was still extant.

In echoes of the successful move by Spalding Urban District Council to restore services on the line from Peterborough in 1970, Oxfordshire County Council with backing from Cherwell District Council, Bicester Town Council and Oxford City Council, in 1986 began an initiative to see passenger services instated.

British Rail's Railfreight sector agreed to a limited passenger service on the basis that it would not transfer any of the track upkeep costs to the passenger operation provided that it could be fitted in around their existing freight services,

Network SouthEast agreed to test the water by running an experimental passenger service from May 11, 1987, to see if there was sufficient demand.

The timetable provided a morning and afternoon peak service in each direction and a late evening service from Oxford on weekdays, with a midday shoppers' service on Saturdays. Off-peak midweek trains were ruled out because five freight trains a day were still using the single-track line, and the signalling could not cope with more.

The trains were popular, but receipts did not cover operating costs. As in cases elsewhere, local councils had to make up the shortfall.

In 1988, Network SouthEast produced a scheme to modify the signalling to allow two trains to use the line between Oxford and Claydon, facilitating six departures from Bicester. A late-night train was added the following year, when on May 13, a single-platform unstaffed station was opened at Islip. Throughout the 1990s the level of service remained basically the same, with variations from time to time as operating and trading circumstances varied.

Since 2005, an enhanced service including Sunday trains has run during the weeks before Christmas,

primarily for passengers travelling to the Bicester Village Shopping Centre next to Bicester Town station. An enhanced service also ran over the weekend of May 12-13, 2007, to celebrate the 20th anniversary since this section of the Varsity Line reopened.

In May 2009, a partnership between then operator First Great Western and Oxfordshire County Council rebranded the line as the Bicester Link. Since December 2008, the county council has been funding improvements to services on the line. Such support was not available in 1963, when the Beeching report was published. Had the enabling legislation of that time been different, even taking into account that many people sincerely believed that the days of the railways were by then numbered in view of the unstoppable rise of car ownership, how many railway services might have survived?

The Mondays to Saturdays timetable was improved with an evening service and a doubling of the number of trains on Saturdays. From May 2009, extra trains were introduced during the daytime on Mondays to Fridays together a new all-year round Sunday service, with a train running every 90 minutes.

ABOVE: Bicester Town station, pictured in 1992, will now be upgraded and enlarged to cope with extra trains once the line to Milton Keynes is open to passengers again. BEN BROOKSBANK*

Between 2007-11, more frequent trains increased the total number of passengers using Bicester Town by 258%, proving beyond doubt that the demand is there. There are now 11 trains from Mondays to Thursdays, 12 trains on Fridays, 13 on Saturdays and nine on Sundays.

Chiltern Railways took over all passenger operations on the line from First Great Western on May 22, 2011.

The rest of the route

In 2013, between Bicester and Swanbourne, the track is in place but overgrown. The section of this length between Bicester and Claydon Junction is used by regular freight trains carrying refuse to the landfill site at Calvert. East of here, between Swanbourne and Mursley, the track has been lifted, but the trackbed remains intact, overgrown but unobstructed.

Between Mursley and Newton Longville, the track is in place but very much overgrown.

The section from Newton Longville to Bletchley was relaid in the spring of 2006 and opened on March 27, 2006, for freight trains accessing the Newton Longville landfill site.

Between Bletchley to Bedford, the route remains in daily passenger use and is marketed as the Marston Vale Line.

East of Bedford, rarely has the formation of a Beeching era closure seen such a variety of second uses – including two very unusual railway systems.

All of the track has long since gone. In summer 2006 it was announced that a large rowing lake would be built near the former station site at Willington near Bedford, in return for a licence to extract gravel. The lake would cut through the route of the trackbed between Bedford and Sandy.

The Bedford Rowing Lake was not ready in time for the London 2012 Olympics as planned, but the £100 million scheme has won support from Olympic rowing champion Tim Foster. Backed by the local council, the scheme aims to also deliver an education campus, a retirement village and a science and technology park, while ending the gravel extraction.

ABOVE: Woburn Sands station on the Marston Vale Line serves the villages of Woburn Sands and Wavendon. This middle section of the Varsity Line, between Bletchley and Bedford, which was opened by the London & Birmingham Railway in 1845, has never closed to passengers despite post-Beeching threats to its existence. Woburn's attractive cottage-type station building, now rented out privately as office accommodation, is one of four of the same design that are unique to this line. At present an hourly service operates each way, operated by either Class 150 or Class 153 diesel multiple units but that is set to change once the Oxford to Bedford route is opened throughout and then electrified. ROBIN JONES

Further east, old station buildings have become homes or been converted to industrial use. At Sandy and Potton new housing occupies the former route.

Between Lord's Bridge and Cambridge, Cambridge University's Ryle Telescope, part of the Mullard Radio Astronomy Observatory, occupies a three mile length of the former route. The giant radio telescopes, which study faraway galaxies, are mounted on a railway built to 12ft gauge. Between Trumpington Park and Ride and Cambridge station the entire route has been converted into the southern part of the controversial Cambridge-Huntingdon Rapid Transit Scheme, also known as the Cambridgeshire Guided Busway.

The longest guided busway in the world, it is a hybrid between the railway concept and the road bus. In this case, concrete guided sections built over former railway formations allow specially-adapted buses to run like trains, at speed and without the need to steer. When the guided section ends, the buses can switch over to 'road mode' and drive through streets in the conventional manner.

The scheme, designed to alleviate congestion on the A14 trunk road, aroused much local hostility, with campaigners saying that the northern section between St Ives and Cambridge (which closed to passengers on October 5, 1970, and was formally closed in 2003) would have been better and more cost-effectively reopened as a conventional railway.

The original cost estimate of £150 million to relay the line as a guided busway rose to £181 million by December 2010.

A new fast line to London

As the years since the Beeching Axe have gone by, there has been increasing pressure to provide fast commuter trains in and out of Britain's capital city. Routes which were then considered to be rural backwaters are now being seen as commuter highways of the future.

Not only that, there have been increasing calls to look again at cross-country routes which do not serve the capital, the focal point of Britain's railways, but link other major centres of population.

In 2001, the Strategic Rail Authority rejected an option to reopen the Bicester-Bletchley route.

However, in April 2006, the Office of the Deputy Prime Minister said it was in favour of

ABOVE: Water Eaton grain silo – the site of the proposed new park-and-ride station to serve Kidlington and north Oxford.

the principle of reopening the link between Bedford and Oxford.

In March 2007, a study funded by councils and businesses found that there was a business case for two trains per hour passenger service between Oxford, Bicester Town and Milton Keynes, as well as over the freight-only former Great Central line from Claydon to Aylesbury. The cost was estimated at up to £135 million.

The East-West Rail Consortium, a group of local authorities and interested bodies along the route, produced a masterplan for the East-West Rail Link, of which the Oxford-Bedford length is regarded as the western section.

The planned middle section from Bedford to Cambridge would use a combination of existing lines together with a new section.

The eastern section beyond Cambridge, running to Norwich, Ipswich and Felixstowe would use existing lines.

In February 2008, the consortium published a business case for reopening the western section of the route. A study was also funded by the Milton Keynes Partnership, the South East England Regional Assembly and South East England Development Agency. It was stated that a 100mph link between Oxford and Bletchley could be achieved for around £190 million.

In April 2008, the Department for Transport responded to an e-petition for support on the reopening of the Varsity Line by restating that it would encourage private funding.

That August, Chiltern Railways, which opened Aylesbury Vale Parkway three miles north of Aylesbury on the freight-only line on December 14 that year, announced radical news plans for a new passenger service between Oxford and Marylebone via Bicester and High Wycombe.

Under the banner of Project Evergreen 3, the proposed services would use the Bicester Link between Oxford and Bicester, where a new half-mile chord would be built to link the Varsity Line to the Chiltern Main Line.

It would give Oxford an alternative to First Great Western's services to Paddington and provide the city with a direct rail link to High Wycombe for the first time since the Princes Risborough-Oxford section of the Wycombe Railway was closed under the Beeching cuts in 1964.

As part of the scheme, Chiltern Railways would redouble most of the line and build a new Water Eaton Parkway park-and-ride station to serve Kidlington and north Oxford. Journey times from Oxford to Marylebone will be under an hour. The scheme also includes upgrades for Islip and Bicester stations.

As part of the scheme, which will greatly intensify the use of the Oxford to Bicester route, Chiltern Railways answered environmental concerns by installing a light system that warns bats about oncoming trains in Wolvercote tunnel near Oxford. Work on the upgrading of the tunnel was halted by a planning inspector in 2011 over concerns about the wellbeing of the bats.

A total of 25 lighting units which will be triggered by approaching trains have been installed inside the tunnel. The idea is that the

ABOVE: *Shannon*, the George England locomotive which ran on the newly-opened Sandy & Potton Railway. ROBIN JONES

ABOVE: A Derby lightweight diesel multiple unit at Verney Junction on March 30, 1965. COLOUR RAIL

ABOVE: The stationmaster's house at Blunham on the Bedford to Sandy section is now a private residence at the heart of the modern Old Station Court development. ROBIN JONES

bats will be alerted by the lights and move to safe crevices in the tunnel walls.

The common and soprano pipistrelle, the noctule and the Natterer's bat are all believed to use the tunnel, which goes under the Wolvercote roundabout on the A40. It is used by bats as a 'flight corridor' to avoid flying over the well-lit road. In May 2013, the £130 million Oxford to Marylebone project was given the final go ahead after an Oxford resident's legal challenge against the Department for Transport's approval was turned down in the High Court. Work on clearing the overgrown parts of the route began in the summer.

Chiltern Railways director Graham Cross said it would be the "first new rail link between two major British cities for 100 years".

Services have been planned using Class 172 diesel multiple units, with Class 165/166s at the outset. Line speeds of 90mph to 100mph are pencilled in between Oxford and Bletchley, 90mph to Aylesbury and the Bletchley-Bedford line upgraded to 70mph.

Onwards to Milton Keynes

Chiltern Railways has long-term aspirations to reach Milton Keynes Central from Oxford, and sees the upgrade of the line to Bicester as an integral first step.

In the 2011 Autumn Statement by Chancellor of the Exchequer George Osborne, the East West Rail project (as it by then had become known) between Oxford, Aylesbury Vale Parkway and Bedford was given the green light, with £270 million of public funding committed to the scheme.

On July 16, 2012, Transport Secretary Justine Greening announced that the western section of East West Rail would be part of the Government's strategy for rail transport.

This western section will link Oxford and Aylesbury to Milton Keynes and Bedford, with the partly-mothballed, abandoned or missing track from Bicester to Bletchley being renewed, with a new intermediate station at Winslow.

Not only that, but the Oxford to Bedford route would also be electrified into the bargain, providing an electric link between the electrified Great Western, West Coast and Midland main lines, and part of the new 'electric Spine' passenger and freight route between the south coast, the East Midlands and Yorkshire.

The project is being developed by the Milton Keynes Partnership together with Chiltern Railways. On January 10, 2013, Network Rail announced its intention to construct the western section between Bedford and Oxford as part of its 2014-19 strategic business plan.

The target date for train services to be operational on this section is December 2017, with one train per hour from Reading to Oxford and Bedford, with the Oxford to Bedford stretch taking 60 minutes, and electrification implemented by March 2019.

On September 6, 2013, a new collaboration between Network Rail and Chiltern Railways was announced. The collaboration will manage the upgrading of the line between Oxford and Bicester Town and the connection of the railway at Bicester to the Chiltern Main Line by construction of the linking spur.

A Network Rail statement said: "The upgrade of the Oxford to Bicester line not only facilitates the new Chiltern Railways service between Oxford and London, but also the first phase of works on the western section of the East West Rail scheme that will reinstate the railway for passenger and freight services through to Milton Keynes and Bedford. Combining the two projects means a more efficient delivery and less disruption for rail users."

Network Rail route delivery director Karl Budge said: "These are exciting times for rail users and the investment being made between Oxford, Bicester and Bedford will make a huge difference to local people and the local economy.

"It makes sense to deliver what were originally separate schemes in a collaborative way. This collaboration will allow fast train services to operate between Oxford and London Marylebone and will move Network Rail closer to reinstating the railway line through to Bedford and Milton Keynes via Bletchley."

Graham Cross, business development director for Chiltern Railways, said: "This collaboration underpins delivery of our new train route between Oxford and London, the launch of which will support economic

growth in the region and benefit thousands of commuters and businesses in Oxfordshire and Buckinghamshire.

"The Oxford to London link is the latest in a long line of innovative Chiltern-specified projects to upgrade the rail infrastructure, fuelled by our understanding of rail's potential to make a significant contribution to UK plc and prosperity. Working with Network Rail ensures we utilise the best expertise to deliver this groundbreaking project."

Coun Janet Blake of Buckinghamshire County Council, chairman of the East West Rail Joint Delivery Board for the Western Section, said: "Enhanced rail services, improved connections and significantly reduced journey times compared to other means of travel will bring enormous benefits to individuals, businesses, communities and the local economy in Oxfordshire, Buckinghamshire, Bedfordshire and beyond."

Many readers will no doubt have been saying much the same since the Beeching Axe was first implemented.

The East West Rail Consortium

Reinstating services from Oxford to Bedford will undoubtedly serve to intensify pressure to reopen the Varsity Line all the way to Cambridge.

The big problem here, however, is the fact that much of the old trackbed east of Bedford is blocked or lost, and a new one would have to be built.

The proposed East-West Rail Link includes the construction of a new nine mile trackbed between Bedford and Sandy on roughly the same alignment as the original. At Sandy, trains would then have joined the East Coast Main Line and run south to Hitchin, from there taking the existing line to Letchworth, Royston and Cambridge.

A chord would be needed to enable southbound trains from Sandy to reach the line to Cambridge, because the existing junction serves only northbound trains from London on to this branch. Cambridge-bound trains from Bedford would therefore not be able to stop at Hitchin unless a new station was built there.

An alternative proposal involves building a new trackbed east from Sandy, thereby avoiding adding to the existing East Coast Main Line traffic. It would continue from Sandy to the east along the original line, skirting Sandy Warren and heading directly east across relatively flat and open country. There could be new stations at Wrestlingworth and Bassingbourn, before the route would rejoin the existing railway network between Royston and Meldreth, leaving the guided busway undisturbed.

If only the Sandy & Potton Steam Railway had got off the ground. Three miles of unblocked track would have been ready and waiting.

Campaign group Railfuture said the jobs, business and improved contacts between academic centres would benefit by extending the line.

Back in the Sixties, it was deemed that with the development of the more versatile road network, there was no place for a slow line between the university cities. Now times have changed, and most people are convinced of the need for a fast service along most of the route. There seems little doubting the multiple benefits that it will bring, and it may be just a matter of time before serious plans to extend back to Cambridge are realised.

Unloved and unwanted for so many decades, the case of the Varsity Line begs the question – how many more routes closed in the Beeching era could offer similar benefits if they were restored?

With the worsening congestion on Britain's roads, it seems that the list will grow longer each year. All it needs is imagination, finance and the willingness of local authorities to become switched on to rail once more.

ABOVE: A single decker runs over the southern section of the Cambridgeshire Guided Busway at Foster Road, Trumpington, once the easternmost section of the Varsity Line. SEAN HICKIN*

ABOVE: The giant radio telescopes which are moved on a 12ft gauge railway laid on the route of the Varsity Line near Cambridge. CM GLEE*

ABOVE: A length of track, a buffer stop and set of wheels have been placed on the east side of Sandy station as a monument to the long-vanished LNWR station built at right angles to the existing one and which served the Varsity Line. ROBIN JONES

Chapter **Sixteen**

The boom town without a railway

It is difficult to find a more clear-cut case for reversing any Beeching cut than the restoration of passenger services to Portishead.

Fifty years ago, Beeching's study indicated that the 10 mile former Great Western Railway could not pay, and accordingly passenger services were subsequently withdrawn.

The Portishead of today is very different to the one of half a century ago, when most of the working population had jobs in the town, primarily in blue-collar jobs.

A 21st century transformation from a workaday industrialised Severnside port to a highly-desirable up-market commuter settlement has seen Portishead become one of the fastest-growing towns in Europe.

However, despite ever-worsening congestion on local roads at peak periods, there are no

train services to gridlocked Bristol, even though Portishead's railway is still in place, a third of it until recently choked by vegetation.

It was GWR architect Isambard Kingdom Brunel who saw the potential of Portishead as a major new port for Bristol Channel shipping.

The estuary of the Bristol Avon is, like that of the River Severn, subject to the second-highest tidal range in the world after the Bay of Fundy in Newfoundland, with the difference between low and high water often reaching as much as 50ft. At low tide, the Avon leading to Bristol becomes a large expanse of glistening mud, which led to the building of the city's Floating Harbour, so that ships could remain afloat throughout the day and avoid damage to their hulls.

Brunel proposed building a pier at Portishead, catering for the bigger cargo

ships of the day. He envisaged it being linked by a branch line to Bristol as long ago as 1839. However, Brunel died before the line was built.

The Bristol & Portishead Pier & Railway Company built a single-track line to Brunel's 7ft 0¼in gauge broad gauge and opened it on April 18, 1867, three years after Brunel's Clifton Suspension Bridge was posthumously completed. In 1861, the town's population was recorded at just 1201.

Hugging the southern slopes of the limestone Avon Gorge, it had three tunnels and stations at Clifton Bridge, Pill, Portbury and Portishead.

The pier at Portishead began operating from 1868, steamers running to Cardiff, Newport and Ilfracombe, and the town's docks opened in 1879.

ABOVE LEFT: GWR 57XX pannier tank No. 3759 calls at Clifton Bridge on March 30, 1958.
T OWEN/COLOUR-RAIL

ABOVE: BR Standard 3MT 2-6-2T No. 82001 at Portishead station on August 22, 1964, shortly before the passenger services were withdrawn under the Beeching axe.
R OAKLEY/COLOUR-RAIL

RIGHT: Bristol & Exeter 4-2-2 No. 48 stands at Portishead station in 1878. The first coach is painted in Bristol & Exeter as opposed to GWR livery. GREAT WESTERN TRUST

The railway, which was at first operated by the Bristol & Exeter Railway, was converted to standard gauge during January 24-27, 1880. It became part of the GWR in 1884, and Ashton Gate station was opened in 1906.

The following year, Portishead became serviced by a second railway, an extension of the Weston Clevedon & Portishead Light Railway, which linked to the GWR branch. It closed in 1940.

The first of two power stations, Portishead A, was opened in 1926. When the new Portishead B power station was almost completed in 1954, the town's main station was demolished to facilitate access, and a modern replacement was built where the Waitrose petrol station

stands today. Both power stations were supplied with coal carried along the branch from the Somerset coalfield, but the bulk of the supplies came by boat from Newport in South Wales.

The branch was closed by Beeching. Passenger services were withdrawn from September 7, 1964 and to standard freight on May 1, 1967. The line remained open for private freight from the town docks until 1981.

As far as Ashton Gate, the home of Bristol City FC, football specials used the line until 1977. Celebrations to mark the 150th anniversary of the Great Western Railway saw the line used for steam specials in 1985, and a run-round loop was specially built in Portishead.

Occasional on-track machines were tested on the branch after 1985 and emergency exercises also took place on the line, as it presented a safe stretch of railway on which to practice, but by 1994, trees were starting to appear between the rails.

However, the closure of the branch to passengers was regretted by local people from the outset, and by 1966, Portishead Town Council was calling for it to be reopened. As with so many other local anti-closure campaigns at the time, the powers that be turned deaf ears.

The new dawn at Portbury

In 1978, however, the Royal Portbury Dock to the east of the town opened. It is a facility of which Brunel would have been proud.

Most of the mothballed branch was reopened at a cost of £21 million for the transport of cars to the docks for export, with the Bristol port company being awarded what was then Britain's biggest-ever rail freight grant, totalling £15.6 million. A new junction was created west of the village of Pill, and a new dockyard freight line built from there to the Royal Portbury Dock.

The 6.5 mile section of the branch from Bristol was resignalled and a long loop to enable trains to pass trains at Bedminster was laid.

The refurbishment works commenced in January 2001 and were completed by the end of November that year. A few days later, a Class 60 diesel was run by

operator English, Welsh & Scottish Railway along the branch and on to the new dock railway.

The guests for the line's official reopening ceremony were taken from Bristol's Parson Street station to Portbury on a train hauled by Bristol Industrial Museum's Avonside 0-6-0ST No. 34 *Portbury* on December 21, 2001.

However, the final 3.3 miles of the original route into Portishead was merely left mothballed, with rampant vegetation claiming more of it by the week. A golden opportunity to restore the branch for passenger use at the time went begging.

Revived fortunes

Portishead A power station closed in 1976 and Portishead B in 1982, Industrial activities ceased at the town dock with the closure of the power stations. The Port of Bristol Authority finally closed the town dock in 1992.

Rather than herald the demise of the town's fortunes, the opposite happened. What to many was a workaday town near the head of the Seven estuary, where the muddy shores did not allow it to take off as a holiday resort like neighbouring Clevedon and Weston-super-Mare, began a transformation into a highly-desirable and fashionable commuter town.

The town's traditional deepwater dock was converted into a marina housing 245 yachts and cabin cruisers. The marina evolved into Port Marine, a very attractive

ABOVE: The name of this large block of luxury modern apartments in the 'new' Portishead recalls the GWR engineer who first thought of building a pier and railway there. ROBIN JONES

LEFT: The Portbury freight line passing beneath Brunel's Clifton Suspension Bridge. Rail revivalists point to the immense tourism potential of a line through the Avon gorge. GREATER BRISTOL METRO RAIL*

waterfront development of luxury apartment and flats built in the style of a fishing village based on Polperro in Cornwall, with narrow streets and multi-coloured houses. New waterside bars and restaurants were opened, and further shops, pubs and restaurants are scheduled to open in the future.

The site of the two power stations has also been redeveloped to provide both social housing, and up-market properties. Major high street stores have moved into the once-downtrodden town centre.

Portishead is now one of the fastest growing towns in Europe, the population being expected to rise to 28,000 in coming years, an increase of more than 350% from 1951 levels, and far greater than when Beeching recommended withdrawal of the passenger services. The large number of new houses, office and light industrial units is set to add 2300 jobs to the existing local market, it has been estimated.

The problem remains – Bristol, a major source of employment for town dwellers, has for decades become increasingly congested, while buzz town Portishead has no railway to access it.

Political pressure

On January 29, 2005, North Somerset MP Dr Liam Fox, the future Conservative cabinet minister, told the House of Commons that the line should be reopened. He said that Portishead was "probably the most overcrowded cul-de-sac in Britain" and that 63% of its adult population travelled out of town to work.

In 2009, a report by the Association of Train Operating Companies stated that the Portishead branch was a special case for reopening due to the large projected increase in population and traffic road congestion in the area. In January that year, Network Rail announced that it would carry out a feasibility study on reopening the line. First Great

Western ran a test passenger train over the useable part of the branch in September 2011, and two months later, delegates to the Rail Priority Conference organised by the West of England Partnership were taken over it.

The partnership comprises four unitary authorities: Bath and North East Somerset, Bristol, North Somerset and South Gloucestershire, along with social, economic and environmental partners, united in the aim of sustaining the prosperity of the region, with emphasis on transport, planning, economic competitiveness, inward investment and skills.

In December 2011, Dr Fox met Transport Minister Norman Baker and expressed hopes that work on upgrading it to passenger-carrying standard could commence by 2015.

In 2012, a 40ft mural costing £6000 and depicting many aspects of town's railway history was erected on land provisionally earmarked for a new station behind the Aldi store in Harbour Road, and unveiled by Dr Fox in April that year.

Jointly funded by the revivalist Portishead Railway Group, Persimmon Homes, Pure Offices and dock developer Crest Nicholson, which owns the site, the mural created by local artist Ali Purdy outlines the railway story of the North Somerset town from the broad gauge days of 1867 to a diesel railcar of 1954 and the anticipated future of the line.

On Saturday, September 29, 2012, First Great Western ran a series of passenger specials from Bristol Temple Meads over the restored section of the branch as far as Portbury Docks.

The case outlined

The Portishead Railway Group says that once the present house building programme is completed, the town will be the largest in Britain without a rail connection, and that a revived line will not only benefit commuters and shoppers travelling into Bristol, but those making the journey the other way into Portishead.

A369, the main road from Portishead into Bristol city centre, becomes gridlocked at times, and some businesses are deterred from relocating to Portishead because of the traffic problems, the group claims.

At present, buses take up to one hour and 15 minutes to reach Bristol Temple Meads station from Portishead. A revived railway could take passengers between the two in 17 minutes, while removing vehicles from roads.

If the branch is revived, it could offer much more to the local economy than carry local passengers, revivalists claim. The spectacular journey through the Avon Gorge could become a tourist attraction in itself, while bringing visitors to the marina. In 2004, Thomas Cook the travel agent listed the Severn Beach line on the opposite side of the gorge as one of the most scenic rail routes in Europe.

Reopening of the entire branch is backed by all local councils, but is dependent on Government funding.

In March 2013, North Somerset Council, which owns the mothballed section of line into Portishead, began clearing the track for a study to be undertaken facilitating design work in advance of a full-scale revival.

In January 2013, the West of England Partnership launched the Bristol Metro 2013 campaign to fight for a half-hourly local train service at all existing local stations and any new ones such as Portishead.

The partnership's campaign was directed at the Government and transport operators ahead of a decision on who should run the Great Western rail network from 2014.

First Great Western pulled out of its existing contract in 2012 to avoid paying £800 million to the Government, but subsequently bidded for the new 15-year contract to run the Great Western franchise.

In June 2013, the partnership asked the Department of Transport for £100 million for its Greater Bristol Metro project, aimed at extending and integrating suburban and

commuter lines in and around the city, and by then rebranded as MetroWest. The submission not only included the reopening of the Portishead branch to passengers but also that of the Henbury loop, a six-mile freight-only line in the north-west of Bristol linking Filton Junction to the Severn Beach line.

The first phase, scheduled to be implemented before 2019, would see a half hourly service from Portishead to Bristol Temple Meads with one train an hour from Portishead going to on to Severn Beach.

A MetroWest briefing note said: "Portishead is key to unlocking MetroWest. Deliver Portishead and the rest of the Metro opens up. This is a major opportunity to deliver a significant change in rail provision in the West of England."

It was said that the scheme would cost an estimated £55 million at 2019 prices.

The schedule for reopening included a detailed business case prepared by the spring of 2014, the submission of a Transport & Works Act order application by autumn 2015, a public inquiry in autumn 2016 if one

ABOVE: This giant mural by Ali Purdy outlines the story of Portishead's transport past and stands on the preferred site for a new station. PORTISHEAD RAILWAY GROUP

is needed, the TWO made in summer 2017, and work starting in late 2017. The work could be completed by April 2019, with the first 21st century passenger trains running out of Portishead a month later.

Yet everyone is asking – why does it have to take so long where there seems to be such a clear-cut case, and the formation is extant and unlocked? A heritage railway revivalist team could surely have the mothballed section up and running within months?

The MetroWest brief explained: "There are technical work streams, planning and regulatory requirements, governance and value for money business cases to work through engineeringwise. MetroWest has to interact with other major rail projects such as electrification, four tracking of Filton Bank (eesential for the hourly service from Portishead to Severn Beach) and the Intercity Express Programme of new electric trains (for the London to Bristol main line).

The Henbury line revival

The Henbury loop is included in the proposed phase 2 of the MetroWest project.

This line, originally named the Avonmouth & Filton Railway was opened on May 9, 1910, as a more direct route to Avonmouth docks. It too closed to passenger traffic in 1964.

In 1971, a curve was opened to link the line to the South Wales Main Line at Patchway, to facilitate traffic to and from South Wales, including zoo excursions to Clifton Down.

A South Gloucestershire Council planning committee

LEFT: The sole surviving coach from the Weston, Clevedon & Portishead Light Railway is this Metropolitan Railway first-class saloon, No. 353, which was built for the Metropolitan Railway in 1892. Rebuilt by the Ffestiniog Railway from derelict condition for London Transport Museum, it was one of the stars of the Metropolitan Railway 150 celebrations which saw steam-hauled public trains return to the London Underground tunnels in 2013. Maybe it could form part of a reopening train for a revived Portishead passenger service? ROBIN JONES

ABOVE: Portsihead has thrown off its once-dowdy industrial port image and is now a highly-fashionable and rapidly-growing commuter town for Bristol. ROBIN JONES

ABOVE: Class 66 diesel No. 65053 heads off the Portishead branch at Bedminster with coal from Portbury. MATT BUCK*

in 2011 recommended that the line be reopened for passenger services. A one-off train operated by First Great Western, ran on the line on July 27, 2013, demonstrating the feasibility of running passenger services over the line, and to make the case for suitable funding.

MetroWest sees the use of the Henbury Line hourly bolt-on service to Bristol Temple Meads via Filton Abbey Wood with capacity for two new stations at Filton North/Henbury alongside the Filton Airfield development.

The last-ever Concorde flight from Heathrow landed at Filton, to be preserved on a temporary apron as a visitor attraction. In April 2011, BAE Systems, the owner of the airfield, announced that the airfield was to close at the end of 2012, with the site being developed for 2500 homes and an aircraft museum to include the Concorde. The airfield was sold off to a London-based property firm for a reported £120 million on the day it closed to flights.

MetroWest said that its business case for the Henbury Line is dependent on the redevelopment of the airfield, as without it there would be insufficient passengers. Should the redevelopment come forward, services on the Henbury Line could start sooner than the predicted 2023 date.

There are calls to extend the electrification of the Great Western Main Line from Paddington to Bristol

Temple Meads to Portishead, the Henbury line, Severn Beach, Yate and Weston-super-Mare.

If all goes to plan, a very bright future awaits railways in and around Bristol. Beeching never saw it coming, but there again, neither did many ordinary people who abandoned the train for the car in his day.

There are many, many people in Portishead, however, who are saying why must they wait until 2019, when, red tape aside, it could be done today, and should have been done sooner.

LEFT: The Portishead branch tunnel at Ashton Gate. STEINSKY*

125

The first train from Bathgate on the reopened line to Airdrie in March 2011. NETWORK RAIL

Going back to go forward

It was around 1982 that passenger numbers on Britain's railways began to rise. Today, we have the highest passenger numbers not only since the Twenties but, some have claimed, in the history of railways, on a network reduced to half of the size that it was long ago in the heyday of the steam era.

Beeching failed to eliminate British Railways' losses before he returned to ICI in June 1965, after producing a second report on February 16 that year, in which he recommended that of the 7500 miles of trunk railway remaining, only 3000 miles "should be selected for future development" – leaving doubts about the future of the rest, including, most controversially, the East Coast Main Line between Newcastle and Edinburgh. He believed that there was still far too much duplication in the system.

The report was rejected by the Labour government. Frank Cousins, the Labour Minister of Technology, told the House of Commons in November 1965 that Beeching had been dismissed by Transport Minister Tom Fraser, who was succeeded by Barbara Castle, a lady who made more cuts without the doctor's assistance. Beeching always denied he had been sacked, stating that he had returned early to ICI as he would not have had enough time to undertake an in-depth transport study before the formal end of his secondment from that company.

Many have said that the phenomenal success of Britain's railway network today has been because of the streamlining and efficiencies implemented by Beeching, and had he never been appointed as chairman, others would have made similar, or maybe even worse, cuts.

Others say he was far too hasty in many cases.

We have come a long way since The Reshaping of British Railways was published half a century ago on March 27, 1963, and have shown that we can look at railways from a multitude of different perspectives rather than solely from the position of an accountant.

Back then, it was an honest attempt to address a problem that presented itself not only in Britain but in other countries where competing road transport was in rapid ascendancy.

It is like shooting fish in a barrel to criticise Dr Beeching and his employers purely with the benefit of hindsight. His planning team did its best to predict up to four decades into the future by analysing the trends of the day, but could not have foreseen the changing social patterns that developed.

The rise of commuter towns and villages tipped the scales, car ownership became more widespread than the planners could have ever dreamt and the population ballooned, among other factors.

The fact is that around the globe, ordinary people stopped using trains and switched to cars, leaving many rural lines seemingly hopelessly non-remunerative, with no apparent glimmer of hope on the horizon that the situation might one day change. In this respect, the decision to close so many lines at this point in history may be seen as justified, in terms of the available criteria of the day.

The biggest mistake, however, and the blame for it cannot be laid at the door of Beeching, was to sell off the vacant trackbeds, or to allow them to be blocked by development. He did not have the remit to demand that they be left intact as possible future transport corridors, whether as roads, bus-only lanes, mass conversion to cycle paths (a later phenomenon), or just maybe, reinstated railways.

As a result, so many mooted rail revival schemes today come up against the stumbling block of major obstacles, such as the long-mooted reinstatement of the Stratford-upon-Avon to Cheltenham route and the difficulty of rebuilding a line through Stratford town centre. This problem is exacerbated by high property values in urban areas, where the expense of buying and demolishing structures to rebuild a railway makes such schemes prohibitively expensive.

In towns and cities where a terminus has been redeveloped and the trackbed lost, there seems little point in reviving the railway, if it means that people would have to catch an extra bus to reach their destination: instead they are likely to opt for the car. When railways were built in the 19th century, urban areas were far smaller, and it was easier to build a town or city centre station. Having to compromise and build a terminus on the edge of a conurbation today will just not do.

The return of the tram

Just as many people in the Sixties foresaw the end of the railway age, a decade earlier street trams disappeared from most of Britain's cities, made redundant by the more versatile bus. Few saw the days when tram and light rail networks would return, but modern trams have the ability to reduce existing vacant heavy rail trackbeds while switching to street running around blockages or to access the heart of city centres.

In 1974, building of the Tyne & Wear Metro began, using former British Rail tracks. The first phase opened to the public in 1980, with extension to South Shields in 1984, Newcastle Airport in 1991 and Sunderland and South Hylton in 2002.

The Docklands Light Railway, a network of driverless minimalist trains, laid on a combination of heavy rail trackbeds and elevated flyovers to reduce the need for land clearance, has been a soaraway success since its first seven mile section opened in 1987, cutting CO_2 emissions and taxi journeys while making a deprived area fashionable. Today, more people are using public transport to access London City Airport than any other airport in the UK.

Its first section opening in 1992, the Manchester Metrolink became the first of the new breed of tramways in Britain, using a combination of heavy rail trackbeds and on-street running, with physical connections to Network Rail.

It was followed by the Sheffield Supertram (1994), the Midland Metro (1999), Croydon Tramlink (2000), Nottingham Express Transit

ABOVE: LSWR7 0-4-4T No. 30052 stands at Cranleigh station with an auto train. The closure of the Guildford (Shalford Junction) to Christ's Hospital (Horsham) line in commuter country on June 14, 1965, under the 'Beeching Axe' is now regarded as a mistake, and loud calls are now being made for its reinstatement. Cranleigh station was demolished soon after closure. BEN BROOKSBANK*

(2004), and after several delays, Edinburgh's tram system is heading for completion.

Revivals and reversals gather momentum

Since the Beeching report appeared, more than 190 miles of track and 350 stations have reopened, mainly through local initiatives which would be been unthinkable or impossible back in 1963.

The main point is that Beeching's figures, though questioned by many, produced evidence that many lines were not paying their way and suggested that they were never likely to do so again. Under modern thinking, such losses can be tolerated if there are perceived additional benefits such as reducing the level of road transport usage and CO_2 emissions in cities, or where providing fast efficient public transport can relieve social deprivation in areas of high unemployment.

Other new routes for passenger trains opened in the past two decades have included the Heathrow Express which opened in 1998 linking Paddington to terminals 1, 2, 3 and 4, the 6.8 mile section of line between Sowerby Bridge and Mirfield, enabling the restoration of a service between Halifax and Huddersfield which was withdrawn in 1970, and the three mile Haughead Junction to Larkhall line on December 12, 2005, which had closed to passengers in 1965 and goods in 1968. With three new stations, the Larkhall-Milngavie service has exceeded all expectations.

On Tuesday, March 8, 2011, Scottish Transport Minister Keith Brown officially opened the Airdrie-Bathgate Rail Link, which had been instigated as part of a set of transport improvement projects proposed by the then Scottish Executive in 2003.

The aim here was to open up a fourth direct railway link between Glasgow and Edinburgh. The project was completed in October 2010, at an estimated cost of £300 million, and reinstates the Bathgate & Coatbridge Railway between Airdrie and Bathgate, closed to passengers in 1956 and to freight in 1982, joining the North Clyde Line of the Glasgow suburban railway network which currently links Airdrie to Glasgow Queen Street station, to the Edinburgh to Bathgate Line, which connects with the West Coast and East Coast Main Lines at Haymarket. It is now possible to travel from Edinburgh Waverley to Queen Street (Low Level) in around 65 minutes.

In London, a major revelation has been Thameslink, an extremely useful north-south link which allows trains from Bedford, Luton and St Albans to pass through the heart of the capital Underground-style, and run on to destinations like Gatwick Airport and Brighton. Advocated by rail revivalist group Railfuture, it was the 1988 reintroduction of passenger trains to a 1½ mile length of freight-only line from Blackfriars to Farringdon from which they had been withdrawn 70 years earlier that provided the simple missing link to make it possible.

A further programme to boost capacity has involved the redevelopment of London Bridge station to create two additional tracks, and a new link at St Pancras will allow trains from Peterborough and Cambridge to use it too, easing pressure on overcrowded services in the South East.

Ones for the future

In the past two decades, there have been numerous calls for redundant rail routes to be revived, either by local campaigners or on a more national level.

In June 2009, the Association of Train Operating Companies produced its report Connecting Communities: Expanding Access to the Rail Network in which it called for the reopening of 14 lines and up to 40 stations which it found that were now commercially viable.

The mooted schemes would be using a mixture of historically closed lines, recently closed or currently operating freight only lines, or sharing heritage railway tracks with permission from their owners.

The schemes included the Birmingham New Street to Walsall via Sutton Park line, which would serve the disenfranchised town of Aldridge and the route from Newcastle to Ashington and Blyth, Aldershot to Borden, with a new station half a mile closer to Bordon than the original one. Then there was Brixham – not reviving the original branch which has been built over, but using the Dartmouth Steam Railway with a park-and-ride at Churston, the South Staffordshire Line from Walsall to Lichfield with new stations at Pelsall and Brownhills, an extension of the Waterloo to Guildford stopping serviced to Cranleigh, with new stations at Cranleigh and Bramley, the Preston to Fleetwood line, with new stations at Thornton and Fleetwood, and Hythe to Southampton via the Romsey to Fawley branch.

In the East Midlands, there would be the Leicester to Burton-on-Trent line, serving Kirby Muxloe, Bagworth, Coalville, Ashby-de-la-Zouch, Moira and Gresley for Swadlincote.

Another heritage line which could play its part would be the East Lancashire Railway, with a new service from Manchester Victoria to Rawtenstall via Heywood.

The report also called for the rebuilding of part of the Brockenhurst to Poole line from Brockenhurst to Ringwood in Hampshire, with a new fast service to London Victoria.

The Skelmersdale branch could be revived to provide a new service from Ormskirk, while the Leamside line in County Durham, once part of the East Coast Main Line, could be rebuilt to provide a fast link from Washington to Manchester Airport.

Finally, the ATOC report listed the Wisbech-March line, which is still intact but mothballed, and currently subject of a heritage rail revival attempt.

Other potential schemes which have long been suggested include the rebuilding of the Southern railway main line from Exeter to Plymouth via Okehampton as a diversionary route for the flood-prone Dawlish sea wall route. The line is still intact from Plymouth to Bere Alston, with the strong possibility of rebuilding it northwards to Tavistock, if a housing development goes ahead, and from Crediton to Meldon Quarry, as the private 18 mile Dartmoor Railway. If Tavistock sees trains again, the reinstatement of the old line from there to Meldon Quarry, which passes low-grade agricultural land on the moorland fringe, would be a comparatively cheap affair, bringing multiple benefits which far outweigh the cost.

Also in Devon, the Tarka Line provides a railhead for North Devon at Barnstaple. Neighbouring Bideford has grown much since it lost its station under Beeching, and yet the trackbed between the pair survives, in use as the Tarka Trail footpath and cycleway. It could easily be rebuilt, while rebuilding the old LSWR line from Barnstaple across the River Taw into the heart of Barnstaple, a flourishing regional centre, and on to Braunton, which now lays claim to be the biggest village in England, and on to Woolacombe and Ilfracombe, would be a far more expensive affair, but could also offer multiple benefits.

How far can the heritage sector help?

In July 2013, the All Party Parliamentary Group on Heritage Rail published its report on the Value of Heritage Railways, in which the question was asked – how far can they go to providing 'real' public transport?

The report stated: "In general, heritage railways provide a tourist ride rather than a public transport service. People come to enjoy the experience of travelling on a steam train, rather than to get from A to B."

It reiterated the point that heritage lines are operated under the Light Railways Act, 1896, with a maximum speed of 25mph. Scope exists to increase this to a higher speed, but any alteration to the terms of operation would take them out of the category of a heritage line, their reason for existence and core business.

Also, fares per mile on heritage lines are considerably higher than the normal bus or national rail fares, reflecting the higher cost of operating steam locomotives and heritage equipment. Heritage railways also largely depend on volunteers who are happy to work conventional day shifts for part of the year, but may not want to work all year round on shifts covering the times required by public transport customers. Accordingly, supplementary paid staff would be needed to fulfil such a commitment, altering the economics of the lines, which would no longer be self supporting, and would need public subsidies.

However, such moves could bring social and economic benefits to a locality, while solving a transport problem. The report continued: "This would be no different from the support payments required by all local National Rail services and indeed, the costs of a service provided by a heritage railway may well be lower.

"While some lines go 'from nowhere to nowhere', others do run in a corridor where a conventional public transport service could be offered. In other cases, the railway could have a valuable 'public tourist transport' role to offer, even if a conventional commuter service would be unlikely to be worthwhile."

Summarising, the report said: "There is clearly some scope to provide a transport service as well as a tourist experience on a number of heritage railways, and the opportunities will increase as the railways extend, particularly where they link with the national network.

"The group considers local authorities should, where justified, encourage the provision of public transport services by heritage railways and that the Department for Transport should consider the benefits of services using heritage railway infrastructure to meet local transport needs, remunerating this, where necessary, through the franchise agreement."

However, experience has also shown that simply reintroducing a year-round passenger timetable on heritage lines will not automatically see local people immediately leave their cars at home and travel to work on the shops by train.

On May 23, 2010, the Weardale Railway, under the direction of principal shareholder British American Railway Services, a wholly owned subsidiary of US company Iowa Pacific Holdings, introduced a timetable including several trips a day between Stanhope and Bishop Auckland using a diesel multiple unit. Within seven months, two of the services had been scrapped. The entire timetable was subsequently axed, along with heritage trains, with the company deciding to focus instead on wine-and-dine trains and special events like its phenomenally successful 'Polar Express' US-style Christmas family attraction, and the coal trains it had successfully reintroduced. In short, it tested the market for regular public

ABOVE: Closures did not end with Beeching or Barbara Castle. The Tunbridge Wells to Eridge line lasted until 1985. Pictured in that year is the final British Rail passenger train, on what would become the Spa Valley Railway, forming the 23.17 Uckfield-Tunbridge Wells West service, arriving just after midnight on July 7. DAVID STAINES

transport, and found that there was no business case at that time.

Elsewhere, two heritage railways might become subsumed back into the national network if another revival proposal ever gets the green light.

The Brighton Main Line 2 Project was established in 2010 to provide a second route between London and the South Coast's premier resort, by rebuilding the Uckfield to Lewes line, which closed in 1969. Part of the route, a mile heading east from Isfield station, is now the Lavender Line.

A second phase of the plan would involve reinstating the Tunbridge Wells to Eridge line which closed in 1985, and has been partially revived as the five-mile Spa Valley Railway. Sufficient compensation would have to be paid for the heritage lines to relocate, with their routes being rebuilt as double track and electrified.

Providing much-needed extra capacity on the Brighton Line, a full reopening would also reduce pressure on the main line into London Bridge via Tonbridge. Network Rail is now looking at the merits of the proposal.

Building new lines

There is little in the Beeching era to suggest that he ever in his wildest dreams thought that one day major new railways would be built in Britain.

The £5.8 billion 67 mile electrified Channel Tunnel Rail Link, or High Speed 1, opened in full on November 14, 2007, providing a high-speed link between London and the Continent, with trains running at up to 186mph. The route had intermediate stations at Stratford International, Ebbsfleet International and Ashford International.

The London terminus is at St Pancras International. The Midland Railway's St Pancras station had become very much the Cinderella of London's termini by the Sixties, when there were several attempts to close it. They were thwarted by strong opposition, with a campaign led by John Betjeman, later the Poet Laureate,

A major transformation in the 21st century saw 'Cinderella' go to the ball, with a new two-deck international station developed within the magnificent fabric of the Victorian original.

Today, the Eurostar journey time from St Pancras International to Paris Gare du Nord is 2hr 15min, and to Brussels-South it takes 1hr 51min. Domestic high-speed commuter services serving the intermediate stations and beyond began on December 13, 2009. DB Schenker operates regular intermodal freight services on the route using adapted Class 92 locomotives, enabling flat wagons carrying continental-size swap body containers to reach London for the first time.

London Underground was the world's first tube railway and has often been described as the best. Indeed, it is hard to imagine how the city would do anything but grind to a standstill if it were ever closed.

Taking the principle into the 21st century is the £15.9 billion Crossrail scheme which, with the building of 26 miles of new tunnels beneath the capital, will link parts of Berkshire and

ABOVE: Work on Canal Tunnels in north London, which run between the East Coast Main Line near King's Cross station and the Thameslink route at St Pancras station, began in September 2013. For the first time, local and regional services from Cambridge and Peterborough will be able to run over the Thameslink route to Gatwick, Brighton, the South Coast and Kent. NETWORK RAIL

ABOVE: Considered redundant in the Beeching era, when several attempts were made to close it, St Pancras is now London's Eurostar terminal, providing a premier gateway to Britain. ROBIN JONES

Buckinghamshire via central London to Essex and south-east London via a high-frequency commuter/suburban passenger service over a 73 mile route.

The services will run from Maidenhead to Shenfield and Abbey Wood, also sharing parts of existing lines with existing services. Ten-car trains will run at frequencies of up to 24 trains an hour in each direction through the central tunnel section.

Services will begin in May 2015 between Liverpool Street and Shenfield and will be extended to other parts of the route during 2018/19, when the central section will come into use.

Finally, half a century after the Beeching report was published, and the British public loudly protested against its recommendations, similar campaigns are underway against the building of a new railway.

The planned High Speed 2 rail link between London, Birmingham, the north of England and eventually the central belt of Scotland has become arguably the most controversial project in the history of Britain's railways.

Britain has long been criticised for failing to follow the lead of other countries and build high-speed lines. While the Beeching closures were taking place fast and furiously, Japan's Bullet trains between Tokyo and Osaka began running in 1964.

Italy followed in 1977 with a high-speed line linking Rome to Florence, and France opened its Paris to Lyon route in 1981.

However, Britain's only high-speed line to date has been the Channel Tunnel Rail Link.

The HS2 project is being developed by High Speed Two Ltd. The line is to be built in two phases, the first being the section between London Euston and Birmingham. North of

ABOVE: A design study of how trains running on HS2 may look. Front wheel faring, the elimination of inter-carriage gaps and shallow raking of the nose cone, will all help to cut the noise generated by the train and also improve its aerodynamic efficiency. HS2

LEFT: An artist's impression of Crossrail's Canary Wharf station. The seven-level structure features a park on top of the passenger concourse and a shopping mall. CROSSRAIL

there, the route would then split into two spurs, one continuing to Manchester Piccadilly, running under Crewe station and Manchester Airport and the other to Leeds via the East Midlands and Sheffield. Other cities are to be accessed using HS2 trains running on existing tracks, or with edge-of-town stations.

In the Sixties, Beeching eradicated the Great Central Railway route as it was perceived as 'doubling up'. Yet, had it been known then that the Channel Tunnel would have been built two decades later, a very strong case would have been made for its upgrading to form part of a route between Britain's industrial Midlands and the north, the capital and the continent.

Many see HS2 as making up lost ground, while also being vital to relieving the pressure on a network that is now stretched to capacity in many areas, the West Coast Main Line in particular.

HS2 promises to cut Birmingham-London journey times from 1hr 24min to 49 minutes, and speeds of up to 250mph will also reduce a Birmingham to Leeds journey from two hours to 57 minutes. Impressive figures for the benefits of HS2 to the regional and national economies have been produced, with many business leaders saying it is of crucial importance.

Yet there have been critics in abundance, and the clamour against HS2 has been steadily growing louder.

Clearly there are mass objections from people living near to the proposed route of the new line, with fears over damage to the environment, devaluation of property prices and the loss of historic buildings amongst the reasons given.

However, there are also increasing concerns as to whether the figures for the economic benefits really stack up.

The project, launched under the last Labour Government, has been supported in principle by the three main UK political parties, and in January 2012 the construction of phase 1 between London and Birmingham was approved by the Conservative–Liberal Democrat Coalition. Construction is set to

begin in 2017 with an indicated opening date of 2026. In January 2013, the preliminary phase 2 route was announced with a planned completion date of 2032.

Yet, where there once seemed to be a greater consensus of political opinion, divisions are blatantly arising, no more so than at the annual Labour party conference in late September 2013. Only days after Labour leader Ed Miliband said: "I support HS2 and I think it's the right thing to do for the country," his Shadow Chancellor Ed Balls told a fringe meeting that if Labour was elected, he would not write a blank cheque to fund HS2 – the budget had by then risen to £42.6 billion, with other estimates placing the true cost by today's prices at £50 billion or more.

He said: "We've got to make it clear we are not going to go ahead regardless. For every billion we spend on HS2 it is a billion pounds we cannot spend on roads, cross-country rail, affordable houses, hospitals and schools."

In August 2013, former Labour Chancellor and Transport Secretary Alistair Darling, who was a Cabinet member when HS2 was promoted by the previous government, warned of a potential "nightmare" on England's railways if HS2 is built. He said that the business case for HS2 has been exaggerated and there are better ways of encouraging growth outside London. He added: "If you build this visionary project, you will have a nightmare on the rest of the network because you don't have the money to spend on it."

Many others have said that the money should instead be spent on improving existing lines and reversing more Beeching closures. Bottlenecks could be removed on the East and West Coast Main Lines to allow faster trains and more frequent services, they claim. HS2 supporters reply that ignoring the lack of capacity now on these routes is burying heads in the sand and allowing Britain to fall further behind.

There is an argument that the reduction in train journey times will be negated somewhat by the need for people to travel additional miles to reach the HS2 stations. Someone living in

south Birmingham, for instance, who wanted to use HS2, would have to make a train journey into the city centre to board a train at the planned terminal in Curzon Street. They might well decide it is quicker to take the car to Solihull or Birmingham International stations and take the longer, and probably much cheaper journey using existing services.

Will people really commute on a daily basis from Leeds and Manchester to London using HS2, or simply relocate nearer to their place of work? In 2012, British Airways introduced five flights a day between Leeds-Bradford International Airport to London. Within a year, the service had been pruned back to 200 seats a day. HS2 will offer 600 seats every half hour.

With the rapid development in digital technology, the number of business executives working at home using broadband is increasing. Within a few years it is likely that it will be possible to view every aspect of an office halfway across the country from a large wafer-thin digital screen hung up on a home study wall. You will be able to see and speak to your staff just as in a traditional office, the only difference being that documents will be sent electronically rather than physically handled.

Beeching, his team and superiors, were inhibited by the fact that they could not see far enough into the future, and the economic circumstances of the day forced them to make honest decisions, some of which were later regretted. To do nothing was not an option.

The same is true with HS2.

Should we shelve it for fear of creating a white elephant which will cripple the existing network, suffering through under investment, or sit back and let the rail system suffer gridlock, potentially pushing people back onto the roads?

Dithering can be similarly destructive, but the divided opinion from informer observers indicates that the HS2 plans as they stand need far deeper scrutiny, even at this late stage.

What is hugely positive, however, is that 50 years after the 'Beeching Axe', rail reopenings and the building of new routes are widely seen as being the way ahead.